A Focus on EU-Russian Relations

Schriften zur Internationalen Entwicklungs- und Umweltforschung

Herausgegeben vom

Zentrum für internationale
Entwicklungs- und
Umweltforschung

der Justus-Liebig-Universität Gießen

Band 15

PETER LANG

Frankfurt am Main · Berlin · Bern · Bruxelles · New York · Oxford · Wien

Kirsten Westphal (ed.)

A Focus on EU-Russian Relations

Towards a close partnership on defined road maps?

PETER LANG
Europäischer Verlag der Wissenschaften

Bibliographic Information published by Die Deutsche Bibliothek
Die Deutsche Bibliothek lists this publication in the Deutsche Nationalbibliografie; detailed bibliographic data is available in the internet at <http://dnb.ddb.de>.

ISSN 1615-312X
ISBN 3-631-54257-7
US-ISBN 0-8204-7756-7

www.peterlang.de

FOREWORD OF THE EDITOR

The Centre for International Development and Environmental Research - [Zentrum für internationale Entwicklungs- und Umweltforschung (ZEU)] - was founded in 1998 as an interdisciplinary and interdepartmental research institute of the Justus-Liebig-University, Giessen. Presently, faculty members from the following disciplines are associated with ZEU: Agricultural Economics, Economics, Environmental Science, Geography, Law and Nutritional Science. Upon ZEU's foundation, the following four sections were established:

Natural resources and environment;

Food security;

Poverty Fighting;

Institutions and development.

These sections also indicate the issues on which research is focused presently. A restriction of ZEU's activities to specific geographic regions is not considered.

The series 'Schriften zur Entwicklungs- und Umweltforschung' [Publications on Development and Environmental Research] - are aimed at the presentation of the results of ZEU's research activities and at the state of discussions in the fields of our research to a broader public. The authors appreciate suggestions and critical remarks in order to reconsider their own positions.

The volumes of the series will appear casually and may be purchased in bookstores or directly from the publisher.

Giessen, May 2005

Professor Dr. Peter Michael Schmitz
Chairman, Board of Directors

Preface

This volume collects revised contributions to the international conference and meeting of the Tempus project between the Université Pierre Mendès France, Grenoble/France, the University of Sussex, Brighton/UK, the University of St. Etienne, the State University of Social and Economic Sciences in Saratov/Russia, and the Justus Liebig University of Giessen/Germany. In May 2004, this conference brought together economic and political scientists of the participating universities. It was held in Russian, English and French. The Russian contributions were translated into English.

The EU and Russia: Towards a close partnership on defined road maps? Without doubt, the EU and Russia have made progress in deepening their relationship. In this respect, the period of 2004/2005 has been a decisive one for the EU-Russian relationship. May 2004 was an important landmark for both Russia and the EU, but particularly for the EU because of its eastern and southern enlargement. A year later, in May 2005, the EU and Russia signed the so-called road maps towards four common spaces. But it still has to be proved whether this ambitious declaration will be implemented, as some of the main conflicting issues and controversies remain. This volume provides an overview of the relationship's status quo, as well as of the challenges and problems both partners have to face. It combines views of scientists from the EU and from Russia with regard to these pressing or latent issues.

First, the volume presents an introductory overview of the EU-Russian relations. In this it focuses on the role of the "energy factor" as a testing ground for the relationship. In the following, the role of the EU as a regional and global actor is evaluated. The internal decision-making processes in the EU are subject of another chapter, as they have sometimes complicated the EU-Russian relationship. Despite 1999's Common Strategy towards Russia, the EU member states have not always found a common position with regard to Russia and the process of decision-making has been even more complicated since the enlargement of 2004. Like a mirror, another chapter considers the global role of Russia and the role mutual perceptions play in the bilateral relationship. In the following chapters the volume examines the prospects for the four common spaces under various aspects. One chapter deals with the impacts and effects of the EU's eastern enlargement on the relationship. The enlargement did have economic, political and psychological effects on the EU-Russian relationship and the negotiations concerning the expansion of the provisions of the Partnership and Cooperation Agreement of 1997 have not always proceeded smoothly. These negotiations have been linked to the negotiations between the EU and Russia on

Russia's accession to the WTO, which are analysed in another chapter. The protocol concerning the WTO accession of Russia has revealed many conflicting issues within the relationship which will also have an impact on the planned creation of the common spaces. Finally, transnational terrorism and the politisation of fear is analysed and put in relation to domestic and external security policies in the EU and Russia. In order to grasp the structure of transnational terrorism, the chapter makes some theoretical observations about the role of fear in national and international politics. In doing so it recognises that fear is an important political and moral force for modern nation-states. In view of current confrontations in Afghanistan, Iraq and Chechnya it becomes obvious that the terrorist threat encourages the politisation of fear in European countries, in Russia and in the US.

I would like to thank Andreas Vasilache for useful comments and his help in preparing the volume. Also, many thanks go to Dr. Matthias Höher for preparing the final manuscript.

Giessen, March 2004 Kirsten Westphal

Content

THE EU-RUSSIAN RELATIONSHIP AND THE ENERGY FACTOR: A EUROPEAN VIEW

KIRSTEN WESTPHAL

1 INTRODUCTION

This paper will analyse the role of Russian energy deliveries to the EU within the overall picture of the EU-Russian relationship.[1] This approach is seen as enlightening as the energy deliveries have been seen and even outspokenly described as the centrepiece of the economic EU-Russian relations. With regard to the political dimension of the relationship, the EU and Germany in particular have faced criticism concerning their policies towards Russia[2]. These policies have been accused of putting stable and secure energy supply at the top of the agenda, while ignoring authoritarian tendencies in Russian policies and pending human rights issues.

In a first step the overall development of the EU-Russian relationship will be analysed from a European point of view, and the quantitative role of energy deliveries in the trade statistics will be described. Secondly, the development of the different policy approaches towards the governing of energy flows will be analysed. It will be shown that there is a mixture and even a discrepancy of approaches towards securing energy trade between the EU and Russia. This lack of coherence and convergence on different levels is not only apparent in the EU-Russian energy relations but is also reflected in the overall level of EU-Russian relations. This determines the hierarchy of the activities in a direction in which day-to-day business and technical questions prevail over long-term strategic issues and over the implementation of ordering principles and legal arrangements. That effect again is reinforced by the Russian policy that prefers to pick and choose the issues to be solved whereas the EU pursues a 'package deal' strategy that aims to create a liberal and transparent market regime. As a consequence, there has not been a break-through towards a common energy space so far, which had been envisaged as early as 1991. The fact that a substantial

1 For their comments on an earlier version of this text, I am grateful to Dr. Susanne Peters and Andreas Vasilache

2 I will use Russia instead of Russian Federation.

rapprochement is hindered by a certain value gap[3] is highlighted in the energy relations, because energy relations in particular demand cooperation and coordination between the EU and Russia, but at the same time reveal the divergence between their positions on a multilateral market and legal regime, on the role of the state in the economy, and on the common neighbourhood. This way, the energy relationship is a real testing ground for the EU-Russian relationship.

2 THE DEVELOPMENT OF THE EU-RUSSIAN RELATIONSHIP

The relationship of Russia with the EU has always been much smoother than that with NATO. Therefore, the EU enlargement has never been an issue of similarly high sensitivity in Russian domestic policy as was the enlargement of NATO. Several factors from the Yeltsin era are responsible for this assumption: The EU was mainly regarded as a trading bloc but was no primary focal point of Russian foreign politics. Instead, the main focus was on the US and NATO, as well as on the so-called 'near abroad' of the former Soviet Union. All in all, the EU as an integration system was not as visible on the radar of Russian foreign policy as were single European member states. This was both a consequence of Russian policies still being fixated on the 'other superpower', the US, or on special partners such as Germany, France and the UK, but also a result of EU policies. After the fall of the Berlin Wall and the dissolution of the Soviet Union, the European member states themselves concentrated on slowly building up the European Union with the Economic and Monetary Union and a Common Foreign and Security Policy. Not only a deepening but also a widening, as well as the enlargement process[4] have bound many political and economic resources.

Yet, for the EU and its member states it was indispensable to look and work out an agenda for the relationship with Russia, as Russia was 'the other pole' in the east of the continent and because of Russia being both a European and an Asian power. Moreover, most of the regional and global challenges such as establishing and maintaining security and stability, nuclear security and non-proliferation, as well as environmental and climate issues among others can only be tackled and solved in cooperation with Russia because of its enormous potential, but also because of its

[3] Value gap refers to diverging norms, diverging setting of norms, and controversies concerning ordering principles such as democratic governance and market order. It does not imply a discussion of values and norms (in a Habermas sense) but perceives it in a broad sense.

[4] For more details please see the contributions of Reimund Seidelmann and Pierre Bailly in this volume.

equally enormous problems which could threaten security and stability on the continent. [5]

In 1994 the EU and Russia signed a Partnership and Cooperation Agreement (PCA) that came into force in 1997. With the newly independent states of the former Soviet Union the EU concluded PCAs in the 1990s. The PCA is a fundamental agreement, concluded for ten years, that structures EU-Russian cooperation and defines the main areas for common activities. It is based on the declaration of common values such as democratic governance, human rights and the commitment to market structures. This way, the PCA established three dimensions of political dialogue, economic cooperation and culture which opened the opportunity to tie the Russian Federation to the European Union and to deepen their relationship. The PCA had a clear emphasis on the political dimension. The "respect for democratic principles and human rights (...)"[6] and the compliance with political conditions, norms, rules, and regulations of the OSCE and the GATT/WTO was defined as a precondition to political and economic cooperation. The reason for the delay in the enactment were the first war in Chechnya and the human rights violations related to the war.

With the EU Treaty of Amsterdam the EU and its member states also strived for more coherence in the Common Foreign and Security Policy and thus adopted a number of foreign policy instruments such as common strategies. A common strategy aims for more coherence in policies and for the implementation of special programmes. At the EU council in Cologne in 1999, the EU adopted the first ever common strategy (a newly created foreign policy instrument) towards Russia.[7] This was a clear sign for the special role the EU attributed to Russia and its importance for stability and peace on the European continent. It expressed the goal to create a *strategic partnership* with Russia.

To sum up and in retrospective, the period between 1991 and 2000 can be characterised as a search for identity and for regional and global roles. This applies to the EU as described above but also and especially to Russia under the presidency of Yeltsin. Whereas the first years of 1992/93 were described as a short period of euphoria and even a 'honeymoon' with the 'West', the relationship cooled down in 1993/94 with a more assertive policy towards the 'near abroad' and a more reserved

5 Shevtsova, Lilia, Putin's Russia, Carnegie Endowment for International Peace: Washington D.C., 2003, p.209.

6 EU-Russian Agreement on Partnership and Cooperation, http://www.europa.eu.int/comm/external_relations/ceeca/pca/pca_russia.pdf (Download 04-29-2005), Art.2.

7 EU Common Strategy on Russia http://www.europa.eu.int/comm/external_relations/ceeca/com_strat/index.htm (Download 04-29-2005)

policy towards the 'West'. Russian public opinion showed an increasing disappointment in 'Western' support which was far less extensive than initially expected. Moreover, the Yeltsin Presidency was characterised by inconsistencies and an increasing personal weakening to which the domestic (the new war in Chechnya and the terror attacks in Russia) and economic situation in Russia with arising social problems contributed to an equal degree. In this regard, the situation profoundly changed during the Putin presidency.

3 IN THE RUN-UP TO ENLARGEMENT AND PUTIN'S FIRST TERM OF OFFICE: TOWARDS A STRATEGIC PARTNERSHIP?

The year 2000 became a crystallising point in EU-Russian relations: The Russian President Yeltsin stepped down on 31 December 1999 and passed on his office to the young Prime Minister Putin. The second Chechen War was used by Putin to present himself as s strong leader and 'holder of the office'. Putin already won the 'post' in the first round of the presidential elections with almost 53 percent on 26 March 2000.[8] This opened a window to restart cooperation.

In general, Putin has developed and strengthened a pragmatic policy course towards the EU since 2000. Putin's foreign policy is characterised by an 'economisation' of Russian foreign policy, which means a reappraisal of the relations with other newly independent states and a re-evaluation of the cooperation with the EU as the main trading and economic partner.[9] This has also been reflected by a medium-term strategy towards the EU that was adopted by Russia as a response to the EU's common strategy.[10] Four factors, which are all interrelated, contributed to this course of policy: 1.) Putin's strong personal position that builds upon rhetoric of an indispensably strong state under the principle of law, efficiency and centralisation of power, 2.) consolidated support for Putin by the Russian public because of a better economic performance (mainly driven by increasing energy and commodity prices) 3.) 11 September 2001 and the 'war on terror' that finally brought Russia back into the international arena as an important partner for the 'West' in both political, as well as security and military terms,

8 For further details see: Shevtsova, Lilia, Putin's Russia, Washington D.C.: Carnegie Endowment for International Peace, 2003, p. 44-103.

9 See: Fischer, Sabine, Russlands Westpolitik in der Krise 1992-2000. Eine konstruktivistische Untersuchung, Frankfurt a.M./ New York, 2003.

10 See: http://www.delrus.cec.eu.int/en/p_245.htm (Download 05/10/05)

and 4.) the run-up to the EU enlargement which would make Russia a neighbour of the EU.

Considering all of this, the years 2000/2001 opened a new window of opportunity for a rearrangement and rapprochement of the EU and Russia. With the common strategy the EU had documented that Russia was seen as a strategic partner and that the member states were interested in a more consistent approach. Putin's strong domestic position made its foreign policy approach more stable and reliable despite the repercussions for the democratic development and the freedom of the media etc. Putin also limited and fought back the influence of strong economic actors such as the oligarchs and strengthened the state's control over important assets such as *Gazprom*, the gas company. Foreign policy instruments and foreign policy agenda settings were regrouped and concentrated by Putin. Putin was also eager and to a large extent successful in linking the war in Chechnya to the problem of international terrorism after 9/11.[11] This is reflected by the fact that western politicians like the German Chancellor were willing to agree on a new formula that acknowledged "that the international community has to come to a more differentiated assessment on Chechnya".[12] As early as October 2000, at the EU-Russia Summit in Paris, the EU and Russia had signed a joint declaration on reinforcing the dialogue and cooperation in the area of security in Europe. This cooperation was strengthened in October 2001 by monthly high level consultations.[13]

Trade and economic cooperation have become more important since 2000. There are even indications that in order to intensify economic links, political conditionality and economic cooperation have been decoupled.[14] Secondly, the EU has made an effort to pragmatically bring economic cooperation with Russia forward and to not stick too much to political conditionality. Moreover, the TACIS programme was restructured and this allowed the support of EU-Russian initiatives.[15] Although the EU's Country Strategy Paper 2002-2006 formulated principal objectives such as 1) the consolidation of democracy, the rule of law and public institutions in Russia; 2) the integration of

11 See the contribution of Andreas Vasilache in this volume which deals with the politisation of fear in Russia and in the EU.

12 Die Zeit, 27.09.2001.

13 Kempe, Iris, Die Europäische Union und Rußland nach dem 11. September, in: Europäische Rundschau, 30. Jhg., 2002/2, p. 107-118.

14 Romanova, Tatiana A., Stanovlenie Evropeyskogo Soyuza kak mezhdunarodnogo aktora (na primere investizionnogo cotrudnichestva ES s Rossiye v energeticheskoi sferye, St. Peterburg: St. Peterburgskogo Universiteta 2003, p.99-120; and Romanova, Tatiana, Energy Dialogue from Strategic Partnership to the Regional Level of Northern Dimension, Draft February-March 2005.

15 Ibid.

Russia into a common European economic and social space; 3) cooperation to strengthen stability and security in Europe and beyond; and 4) the addressing of common challenges for the European continent, e.g. the environment, nuclear safety and the fight against crime[16], economic cooperation and trade matters were moving upward in the hierarchy of the agenda. One sign was that the EU acknowledged the market-economy status in 2002, for which Russia had been pushing for a long time in order to start negotiations on joining the WTO. This encouraged Putin to define the creation of 'a single economic space' with the European Union as an objective. An idea that was translated into the 'four common spaces' at the St. Petersburg EU-Russia Summit in May 2003. The common spaces were defined as

1) an economic space,
2) a common space of freedom, security and justice,
3) a common space of cooperation in the field of external security and
4) a common space of research and education, that also includes culture.[17]

This formal declaration had to be filled with substance and this proved to be more complicated. Already the bilateral negotiations between the EU and Russia on a protocol for the accession of Russia to the WTO revealed conflicting positions which lay beyond the general commitment to strengthen the cooperation. The EU raised the crucial issues of the application of international WTO standards, the opening of Russian markets and their liberalisation with a special focus on the energy sector and the still regulated gas prices.[18] These more penetrating questions disclosed profound dissension between the two partners on how and whether to institutionalise and structure a 'common economic space'. Practical policy questions emerged, which had implications for both the approach of EU policy and for the EU-Russian relations.

The EU emphasised the "considerable interest to engage and build a genuine strategic partnership on the basis of positive interdependence."[19] This formula of a *positive interdependence* clearly hints to the EU pattern of expanding the space of stability by promoting trade and economic cooperation. In the EU integration process this has gone hand-in-hand with the export of political principles and institutions (Criteria of

16 CSP 2002-2006, National Indicative Programme 2003-2003, Russian Federation, p.3. http://www.europa.eu.int/comm/external_relations/ceeca/com_strat/russia_99.pdf (Download 04/29/2005)

17 EC, Communication from the Commission to the Council and the European Parliament on relations with Russia, COM (2004) 106, 09/02/04, p.1.

18 For further detail see the contribution of David Dyker in this volume.

19 EC, Communication from the Commission to the Council and the European Parliament on relations with Russia, COM (2004) 106, 09/02/04, p.1.

Copenhagen) and the enlargement of the range of legal force, a somewhat legislative approach (*Acquis Communautaire*). Beyond the cases of candidate countries, the EU seeks to follow a similar pattern of gradual integration and of accompanying commercial relations with the export of norms, rules and institutions as formulated under OSCE patronage, or in the economic field along GATT/ WTO principles, legislative cooperation and even legal harmonisation in the sphere of market(s) and sectoral organisation.

This pattern is also reflected in the European Neighbourhood Strategy Paper of May 2004[20] and the European Neighbourhood process as outlined since 2003, which is directed to the neighbouring countries of the east and the south. The European Neighbourhood Policy is a foreign policy instrument applied to a region of vital interests for the EU. The Neighbourhood Policy was initiated on the eve of enlargement to define principles and guidelines for the neighbouring countries without opening a short or medium-term 'track' to accession for them but in order to integrate them into a space that is dominated by stability, security, democratic principles, and human rights and social prosperity. The EU Neighbourhood Policy explicitly includes Russia without giving clear guidelines on how to define a special role in comparison with the other countries addressed in the post-Soviet space such as Ukraine, Moldova, Belarus, and the South Caucasian states. The ENP cannot distract from the fact, however, that the EU has always given priority to the EU-Russian relationship.

However, the EU has also addressed concerns about the internal developments in Russia. An EU assessment report of February 2004 stressed the importance of cooperation with Russia in different spheres such as stability and well-being in Europe, security and environmental issues etc., and emphasised the necessity to bring the partnership with Russia forward, while also reflecting on arising disagreements. For instance, the communication explicitly mentioned that the period since 2000 and during Putin's presidency "witnessed a weakening of values to which the EU and Russia (as a member of the Council of Europe and the OSCE) are committed (...)".[21] Moreover, the communication referred to the way the Duma election was conducted in 2003, the situation in Chechnya and indications of selective application of law in Russia. The 'value gap' between the EU and Russia became more pronounced in 2003 and questions were raised with regard to "Russia's commitment and ability to uphold core universal and European values and pursue democratic reforms."[22]

20 EC Communication COM(2004) 373 final, Brussels, May 2004.

21 Ibid., p.2.

22 Ibid.

4 THE CURRENT RELATIONSHIP: A STRATEGIC PARTNERSHIP BASED ON COMMON SPACE(S)?

Despite some positive developments in 2004/2005 the EU-Russian relationship has not qualitatively proceeded; rather, divergent interests and perceptions have become even more evident. The EU-Russian relations have become more complicated because of internal developments in the EU related to the enlargement, because of divergent views between the EU and Russia concerning the common neighbourhood, and because of internal developments in Russia.

The year 2004 witnessed another move towards a centralisation of power under president Putin. The parliamentary election in December 2003 already earned almost 40 percent and a constitutional majority in the Russian state duma for the 'party of power', the party *"Edinaya Rossiya"*. Putin's position was again strengthened when on 14 March 2004 over 71 percent voted for him in the presidential elections.[23] On the surface, this meant continuity and stability for the EU-Russian relations as Putin's strong position and the centralisation of power made foreign policy more reliable and stable, especially in comparison with the Yeltsin years. Yet, this did not make policies more democratic.

The signing of a common protocol on the questions concerning the Russian application for an accession to the WTO in May 2004 is one of the steps forward. On the one hand, the long negotiations revealed the controversial issues, on the other hand it became evident that the protocol was seen as a centrepiece of a package deal. The most controversial issues were the liberalisation of the Russian market and especially the gas, banking and telecommunications sector, as well as tariffs.[24] It was agreed upon the application of the Partnership and Cooperation Agreement provisions to the enlargement of 1 May 2004 with ten new eastern and southern European member states and the application of certain trade preferences to Russia.[25] These negotiations on trade issues were closely related to the bilateral EU-Russia negotiations on Russia's WTO application.

Related to the EU enlargement of ten new member states on 1 May 2004 is the Kaliningrad question, in the case of which both sides have so far not come to an arrangement which is satisfying for both sides. With the accession of Poland and the three Baltic states Kaliningrad has become a Russian exclave within the territory of the EU. This has raised a number of issues. The visa and transit question have been most

23 Zagorski, Andrei, Putins zweite Amtszeit, in: Russland-Analysen 48/2004, p.2-5, p.2.

24 Pleines, Heiko, Der Moskauer EU-Russland Gipfel, in: Russland-Analysen 28/2004, p.2-4.

25 For the impacts of the enlargement on the EU-Russian relationship see the contribution of Olga Garanina in this volume.

prominent in public. Socio-economic issues, however, are yet to be solved as well: A legitimate Russian concern has been the special geographical and economic situation of the Kaliningrad region between Poland and Lithuania, as it has no direct access to the Russian Federation. This causes very special challenges for the socio-economic development and for the balancing of both aspects to neither allow a deep socio-economic gap between Kaliningrad and its EU neighbours, nor a huge heterogeneity with the Russian Federation, which might question Russian territorial integrity.[26] Russia has always emphasised the fact that the Kaliningrad region is a part of the Russian Federation and that the territorial integrity of Russia has to be considered in all dealings with the enclave. In order to meet these challenges Russia suggested in its Middle Term Strategy towards the EU (2000-2010)[27] to transform the Kaliningrad region into a pilot region for the EU-Russian cooperation, but since then it has done little to give this plan any substance.[28] The EU has not picked up this proposal either.

Another issue that has put a strain on the relationship since 2003 has been the *Yukos* affair, which on the one hand has been increasingly seen as being in line with a renationalisation of the oil industry, and an authoritarian consolidation of vertical state power on the other hand. Even if the interpretation as a 'master plan' might be exaggerated, the *Yukos* case however stands as an example for these developments.[29] Mikhail Khodorkovsky, the chief executive of *Yukos* had supported civil rights groups and had sought to attain more influence in Russian politics as well as taken over the liberal newspaper *'Moskovskye Novosti'* in 2003, the year of the election campaign. This prompted reactions from Putin and his administration as they sensed the appearance of an oligarch who was also looking for political influence. After the experiences of Yeltsin's second term in presidency Putin has striven to contain and cut back the influence of the economic elite since 2000. The warning signals of Khodorkovsky's arrest were not only directed towards the political opposition but also towards the business elite with a clear hint not to act against the Kremlin's line and to

26 For further detail see: Birckenbach, Hanne-M./ Wellmann, Christian (eds.) The Kaliningrad Challenge. Options and Recommendations, Münster 2003.

27 Russia's Middle Term Strategy towards the EU (2000-2010), http://www.delrus.cec.eu.int/en/p_245.htm (Download 04/29/05).

28 Birckenbach, Hanne-M., Für ein europäisches Haus in Kaliningrad, in: SCHIFF-Texte 72, Dec. 2003, p. 4.

29 As the concerns about renationalisation will be subject further below in the analysis of the 'energy factor', which will also link this case to new legislative projects, revision of oil producing projects with foreign partners and planned mergers, the article will at this point focus on the political signals given to the political opposition and to business.

fulfil tax payments.[30] In the *Yukos* case the West has criticised Russia harshly for a selective application of the law. Especially the Council of Europe has investigated and reported the case. Not only the *Yukos* case and its political implications, but also Putin's efforts to strengthen the vertical power after the tragedy of Beslan has heightened concerns in the West about a more assertive and authoritarian political course.

A growing gap between a 'wider Europe' and a 'wider Russia' opened with the developments in the common neighbourhood with the so-called 'Rose Revolution' in Georgia and the 'Orange Revolution' in Ukraine. Since the dissolution of the Soviet Union, Russia has offered many different integration schemes to the newly independent states in order to maintain its sphere of (political and military) influence in the 1990s. The economisation of Russian foreign policy under Putin brought about new integration efforts directed towards economic cooperation. In all integration attempts since 1991 the Ukraine played a pivotal role for Russian policy because of the factual and psychological meaning the country always has had for Russia. The reorientation and strengthening of the 'western vector' in Ukrainian foreign policy has always been a highly sensitive issue for Russia. Russia has exerted influence on the gas tap in order to pressure Ukraine to join integration efforts. On the other hand, Russia has successfully tried to step by step reduce its dependence on Ukraine as a gas transit country. A significant step to reduce the amount of gas exported to Europe through Ukraine was the Yamal pipeline, and the planned Baltic pipeline will be another significant step as it links Russia and Germany directly.[31] But the EU also implemented a common strategy on the Ukraine half a year after the first ever EU common strategy had been developed for Russia.[32] This highlighted the special position of Ukraine. The 'wider Europe concept' somehow offered an alternative to the 'wider Russia' integration efforts in the Eastern European region.

Particularly the situation in Ukraine which flared up with the elections in November/December 2004 has functioned as a crystallising point. The EU and Russia found themselves in diametrically opposite positions. From the beginning of the campaign Russia openly supported the candidate of the establishment, Yanukovich, whereas the EU later backed the opposition's candidate Yushchenko. The EU and

30 For a very good and detailed description and analysis of the Khodorkovsky case see: Gernot Erler, Der Fall Chodorkowskij – Zur Tomographie eines politischen Konflikts, in: Gabriele Gorzka/ Peter W Schulze, Wohin steuert Russland unter Putin?, Der autoritäre Weg in die Demokratie, Frankfurt: Campus, 2004, S. 301-325.

31 Rar, Aleksandr, Itogi Gannovera – plokhaya novost' dlya Yushchenko, in: Neftegazovaya Vertikal' – Novostnaya Lenta 12.04.05.

32 See: http://www.europa.eu.int/comm/external_relations/ceeca/com_strat/index.htm (Download 04/15/2005)

Russia found themselves on different sides; the EU backed the OSCE reports[33] which questioned the fairness of the campaigns and the results, whereas Russia represented the diametrical position and supported the officially announced results of the elections and declared the elections as free, fair and legitimate on the basis of the judgement of election observes sent by Russia and the Commonwealth of Independent States. The clash of EU-Russian positions also reflected two concepts of integration in the region which are increasingly competitive. Russia supported Yanukovich as the candidate who was seeking a closer relationship or at least a status quo with Russia, whereas the EU backed Yushchenko who postulated further reforms and a orientation towards the 'West'. The election in December 2004 has changed the situation profoundly, because the 'European vector' will be strengthened significantly. Also, the Yushchenko/Timoshenko leadership will have to balance policies between the strong ties with and dependencies upon Russia and powerful oligarchic groups in the east ,and the wish to join the EU.[34]

The clash of EU and Russian positions also complicated the procedures in the OSCE, which both partners are members of: Russia temporarily stopped its payments to the budget. In reaction to that the EU thought of stepping in with financial support. What has become very clear in the dispute is that Russia did not block the contribution for financial reasons but because "(i)t [was] a question of principle", as the Russian ambassador to the OSCE stated.[35] The perception of the Russian government is that it sees the OSCE as acting against Russian interests as reflected in conflicts concerning elections in Chechnya, Georgia, Belarus, Ukraine and recently in Kyrgyzstan. Russia has tried to exercise pressure on the OSCE to make it shift away from election observation, democratic and human rights issues and human security to an approach that is based on traditional security and military issues as well as on economic issues.[36] Problems are now imminent because the future contributions to the budget and the priorities will be re-negotiated in autumn 2005.[37]

The Ukrainian case has also strengthened the influence of the new member states on EU foreign policy towards Russia. At first, it was Poland and Lithuania which got engaged in the Ukrainian case and adopted a clear contra position to Russia. Only

33 See: OSCE, Statement of Preliminary Findings and Conclusions on the First and the Second Round: http://www.osce.org/odihr-elections/documents.html?lsi=true&limit=10&grp=220 (Download 04/15/2005)

34 Fischer, Sabine, Rußland und die Ukraine, Fehlkalkulation oder neoimperialer Impuls?, in: Osteuropa, 55Jg., 1/2005, p.64-76.

35 International Herald Tribune, 29 March 05, p.8.

36 Ibid.

37 International Herald Tribune, 13 May 05, p.3.

later the EU and the High Representative Solana became active. Particularly the problems between the Russian and the Baltic states have a detrimental effect on EU-Russia relations. This has become apparent at the EU-Russia summit on 1 May 2005 when the two partners finally signed the 'road maps' for the four common spaces[38] but when the disputes on formal territorial treaties between Russia and Latvia, and Russia and Estonia overshadowed the event.[39] The adopting of the road maps was a formal success that seemed to be inspired by the 60th anniversary of the end of World War II and the wish to carry the spirit of the celebrations further. This paved the way for an agreement, but it is questionable whether the road maps will provide a smooth trip towards the common spaces; it might also turn out that these are road maps to nowhere.

It was only in November 2004 that a summit did not bring forth any substantial results on the four common spaces of economy (including energy and environment), of freedom, security and justice, of cooperation in the field of external security and of research and education, which also includes culture. The positions on general issues as well as on technical details were too divergent: The EU pursued a consistent and coherent approach that linked the four spaces and wanted to negotiate a package deal. Opposed to that, Russia followed a 'pick and choose' strategy fitting to the Russian interests.[40] The least controversial space on the November summit was the space of research and education. As for the common economic space the Russian side showed reluctance to adapt parts of *Acquis*, which represents 'international best practice' and rather seeks a pragmatic approach. The common space of freedom, security and justice was almost blocked by controversies over Chechnya, the situation of the media in Russia and the situation of the Russian minority in the Baltic states. The general positions within the field of external security were not that different from each other but Russia rejects the EU proposal to make the common neighbouring countries such as Belarus, Ukraine, Moldova and Georgia a focal point.[41] For Russia the latter has been a sensitive question that touches upon its claim for leadership in the former Soviet Union. These differences of opinion have not been cleared up yet. Therefore it will have to be seen whether the 'road maps' will be operationalised and implemented in the near future. Without doubt the signing is important because the PCA will end in 2007, but the controversies remain and the formal declarations of intent cannot hide the fact that there has been very little substantial progress. The most apparent

38 See the files: http.//europa.eu.int/comm/external_relations/russia/summit_05_05/index.htm (Download 05/11/05).

39 IHT, 05/11/05, p.3.

40 Meier, Christian, Nach dem Gipfel von Den Haag, SWP aktuell 58/ Dez. 2004.

41 Ibid.

indication for this is that the two partners could not agree on a new visa regime or on a timeframe for the implementation of technical cooperation projects.[42]

On the whole, the relationship has reached the critical point whether or not to bring the strategic partnership forward and whether or not to implement the common spaces. The question is very much whether a coherent approach towards a positive interdependence can be achieved. The EU perceives Russia as a strategic partner but has made it clear in the 'wider Europe concept' that it sees Russia in the context of the common neighbouring countries. Russia in turn seeks an exclusive partnership with the EU and wants to be at least the *primus inter pares*. Russia wants to build up the partnership selectively and focus on important issues of policy rather than seek an overall, transparent and equally applicable framework. This is a policy which has prompted Russia to seek closer and selective bilateral ties with the big member states such as Germany, France and Italy. This trend may prove to intensify when the new eastern member states obtain more influence on EU foreign policy and contribute their engagement with the neighbour states the way Poland did in the Ukrainian crisis.

At this point it is enlightening to turn to the 'energy factor' and the EU-Russian energy relations as a major focal point of the overall relationship.

5 A PICTURE OF EU-RUSSIAN TRADE RELATIONS AND THE SHARE OF ENERGY

For hydrocarbons the EU relies on a few main suppliers which cover two thirds of all supplies. Its own production of hydrocarbons will have decreased by roughly 20 percent until 2020, whereas the demand will increase in the same period. The overall energy dependence in the EU is expected to increase to up to 70 percent by 2030. In the case of oil dependence it could reach 90 percent, for gas 70 percent, and for coal 100 percent. This trend has been reinforced by the enlargement, especially for oil and gas. Despite these preoccupying trends, the EU has been reluctant to make strategic long-term provisions.

Russia is a strategic if not the energy supplier of the European market: 34 percent of the oil exported to Europe comes from the former Soviet Union, the major part from Russia; the gas imported from Russia amounts to 43.9 percent. The share of Russian

42 NZZ Online, Schatten über dem Russland-EU-Gipfel, 05/11/2005 und NZZ Online, Russland-EU-Gipfel ohne greifbare Resultate, 05/11/2005; Http:/www.nzz.ch/2005/05/11/al/articleCT1EI.print.html (Download from 05/11/2005).

gas imports will increase to up to 70 percent for the EU-30.[43] Russia and its Western Siberian gas fields will also be crucial for the supply of the EU with natural gas. Gas consumption is likely to increase in the EU, first because gas is a cleaner energy source with a lower carbon dioxide emission than coal, and also because several regions in the EU will be linked to a gas pipeline system because of environmental concerns. Along the so-called Prodi Plan of September 2000, gas imports from Russia will double to 240 billion cubic meters until 2020. This implies that Russia is the EU's biggest supplier of hydrocarbons, followed by Norway and Saudi Arabia for oil and Norway and Algeria for gas. This way the EU is in breach of the rules agreed upon at the G7 summit in 1983, which laid down that energy imports from a single source, respectively a country, should not exceed 30 percent of the overall imports. This share of energy imports also means that the EU is structurally dependent on Russia as an energy supplier, as a large share comes from a single source and is transported through only a few pipelines - a dependence which is likely to persist or even to increase. By the year 2020, the Russian share of EU-30 oil imports will slightly decrease, but Russia will still be the main single source.[44]

It may be argued however, that the overall picture of trade is rather one of mutual interdependence than one of structural dependency. Export revenues obtained from oil and gas account for roughly 40-45 percent of the budget. The oil sector accounts for 25 percent of the Russian GDP[45]; if the gas sector is included this share rises up to more than 35 percent. Russia sells 53 percent of its oil exports and 62 percent of its gas exports to European Union member countries. More than 80 percent of all exports are natural resource-based, of which oil and gas make up nearly 60 percent.[46] This makes Russia vulnerable to volatile energy prices. Moreover, the EU is now by far Russia's main trading partner. The EU-15 already accounted for about 37 percent of Russia's overall trade. This figure could go up to 50 percent after the EU enlargement. The EU-Russian trade structure is unbalanced, with mineral fuels accounting for 60 percent of EU imports in 1999, while machinery and transport equipment represent around 40 percent (and food 15 percent) of EU exports.[47] This means that reliance on natural

[43] The EU-30 encompasses the new member states, the candidate states, and Norway and Switzerland (Götz, Roland, Rußlands Erdgas und die Energiesicherheit der EU, SWP Studie 12/ April 2002, p.16).

[44] Götz, Roland, Die russische Energiewirtschaft und die Energieversorgung Europas, in: Gorzka/ Schulze, Wohin steuert Russland unter Putin? , S. 87-115, p.99.

[45] IHT, 04/15/05, p.3.

[46] EC, Communication from the Commission to the Council and the European Parliament on relations with Russia, COM (2004) 106, 02/09/04, p.10.

[47] European Commission, Country Strategy Paper 2002-2006, National Indicative Programme, Brussels, 12/27/2001, p.4.

resources is too high and shows that Russia's economy is not sufficiently diversified. Moreover, the Russian imports from the EU illustrate the need for a restructuring and improved competitiveness of the Russian industry. Furthermore, the Commission emphasises the great potential for EU exporters and investors, as, given the low level of living standards in Russia and the size of its market, there is great potential if the framework of the market economy and the investment climate can be improved and steady economic growth can be achieved.[48] These trade figures have to be considered as contributing to a more balanced picture of interdependence.

But still, the current huge trade surplus of Russia obtained by trading with the EU illustrates the EU's continued dependence on energy supplies from Russia. Moreover, Russia has consequently diversified its energy exports to other world regions since 2000. A major step towards unilaterally decreasing the dependence on Europe as a buyer of energy sources was the oil partnership of Russia and the US, signed in 2000[49], which may soon be supplemented by a partnership on natural gas. This energy partnership might start a competition between the EU and US on Russian energy exports. In any case it puts a higher pressure on the EU. Furthermore, Russia has committed itself to deliveries to Japan and China. This again strengthens Russia's bargaining position with regard to the EU, as it provides Russia with a spectrum of possible buyers for Russian hydrocarbons. This argument is even more important in connection with the growing consumption world wide. Moreover, the physical capacities of Russia to fulfil all the contracts concluded are to be questioned, as the major production sites have already reached their peak of production and not that many new sites have been opened in the course of the 1990s.[50]

Below, it will be argued that the question whether the energy deliveries from Russia are creating a mutual interdependence rather than a structural dependence is entailed to a high extent by the existence of a framework and of ordering principles the two partners are setting up in order to achieve mutual predictability, stability and transparency.

48 European Commission, Country Strategy Paper 2002-2006, National Indicative Programme, Brussels, 12/27/2001, p.4.

49 See: Victor, David G./ Victor, Nadejda M., Axis of Oil?, in: Foreign Affairs vol. 82, No. 2, March/ April 2003, p.47-61.

50 See: Götz, Roland, Russlands Energiestrategie und die Energieversorgung Europas, SWP Sudie 6, März 2004.

6 EU-RUSSIAN ENERGY DIALOGUE

In comparison with other energy rich and energy producing countries - mostly Arab countries - Russia is perceived by and in the EU as a reliable and stable energy supplier because of the fact that Russia is an alternative energy supplier outside the OPEC - also because it has steadily and uninterruptedly delivered gas to West Germany since the 1970s.

At an EU level, the level and structure of external dependence was first and explicitly made subject of the discussion during the preparation of the Green Paper 'Towards a European strategy for the security of energy supply' in autumn 2000.[51] Autumn 2000 in general was an important mark in EU-Russian energy relations because the President of the EU Commission announced the Prodi Plan and the EU-Russian Energy Dialogue in September 2000. The Energy Dialogue started in September 2000 and is conducted *ad personam* by vice premier Victor Christenko on the Russian side and by the General Director for Transport and Energy in the Commission, Francois Lamoureux on the side of the EU. As described above, this fell together with the overall developments. But the Green Paper has also heightened the awareness of the importance of energy deliveries from Russia. Energy cooperation moved upwards on the agenda of the relations.

The EU-Russian Energy Dialogue[52] has a two-fold objective: First and foremost it is designed to gear the flows of energy trade and investment and to overcome certain antagonisms between the two differently structured markets. Secondly and as a desired side-effect it is a mechanism to adjust European positions in the dialogue with the main energy trading partner. Last but not least the dialogue was directed at developing the 'energy partnership' in order to achieve a win-win situation of mutual advantage. Therefore, the dialogue was organised as a multi-level attempt to govern energy relations by integrating all participants from the political and the economic side into the several working groups and round tables. Furthermore, a common energy technology centre was opened in Moscow and a market observation centre is planned in Brussels. The EU and Russia have defined short and long-term issues for the Energy Dialogue which can be divided into four overarching themes:[53]

51 Commission of the EC, Green Paper - Towards a European strategy for the security of energy supply, COM (2000)769final, Brussels, November 2000.

52 See the Progress Reports of the Energy Dialogue: http://www.europa.eu.int/comm/energy/russia/overview/index_en.htm

53 The following is adapted from the Communication (2004) 777 final, The Energy Dialogue between the European Union and the Russian Federation between 2000 and 2004, Brussels 12-13-2004.

1) Internal market: The transparency of the markets and competition as a guarantee for a stable EU supply are emphasised under this theme. Some related short-term issues such as the question of the long-term contract and the abolishment of destination clauses are already solved by now.

2) Sustainable development: A related short-term issue was the ratification of the Kyoto Protocol as well as pilot projects on energy saving in Archangelsk, Kaliningrad and Astrachan. A major issue here is a safe infrastructure network. This is an especially sensitive issue for the littoral states of the North and the Baltic Sea.

3) Predictable and stable supply: Supply security has to deal with certain risks and challenges related to dependency on external energy supplies. Apart from the short-term issues of transport infrastructure and trade in energy products this is directed to a relation of constructive interdependence which is based on predictable trade rules and a more transparent and stable legal framework. Trade in energy products encompasses nuclear material. A gas pipeline through the Baltic Sea, which links the UK with Russia via Germany has been defined as a priority axis within the trans-European networks.

4) Smoothing the way towards market harmony across the continent: An interconnected electricity network is being pushed most strongly. This long term objective reflects the need for shared principles between the two markets. Among the long-term issues is the joint use of the two satellite navigation systems GALLILEO and the Russian GLONASS in order to reinforce the safety of infrastructure and production. Another objective is to provide investment guarantees because the investment climate in Russia has to become more transparent, stable and predictable to meet the high investment needs; also in order to develop new production sites to meet the growing European demand.

From the side of the EU the Energy Dialogue with Russia is about much more than about increasing imports from Russia. It has been seen as a component to *positive interdependence* which not only builds upon physical trade and financial flows from both sides, but also *constructively* builds upon a common definition and implementation of norms and rules up to legally binding arrangements, which are highly valued by the EU. Consequently the EU has been pushing for regulations and the application of international law in order to facilitate trade, commerce and investments in the energy sector. The dialogue is geared towards establishing a common regulation scheme or even one common market for energy. Of course, this approach is also aimed at allowing western companies full access to the Russian energy market, but it is a crucial element to secure energy supply to Europe.

The EU has sought to export its own approach towards increasing energy security by linking it to climate and environmental protection. This way the effectiveness of energy use and energy savings is an element of the dialogue. As the Russian ratification was crucial for its coming into force after the US withdrawal the EU pushed Russia to ratify the Kyoto Protocol. Without doubt the ratification of the Kyoto Protocol by Russia on 22

October 2004 was a landmark in the Energy Dialogue, in the bilateral relationship and a sign that the *do ut des principle* and the wish to produce a mutually beneficial situation worked in the bilateral negotiations on Russia's WTO accession - the EU had already signed the protocol in May 2004.

The Russian side has pursued different interests in the EU-Russia Energy Dialogue. Russia itself has intertwined the dialogue with the EU's support of Russia's bid for accession to the WTO. First and foremost Russia was interested in maintaining and securing its strategic position as the major single energy supplier to the EU. With this objective, Russia has put pressure on the EU to extend the acceptance of long-term contracts despite the fact that this was contradictory to the liberalisation of the European gas market. Initially, the EU had wanted to increase the position of 'spot markets for gas'. Because of the structural characteristics of the gas infrastructure and the huge investments which have to be undertaken to build pipelines the EU finally accepted the Russian arguments.[54] In turn Russia had to relent its position on the destination clause that was originally linked to the long-term contracts in order to determine the destination of the gas sold to the EU and to avoid a re-selling on the EU market. Russia exerted pressure on the EU to give up any plans of limiting imports to the EU or to member states from a single non-European supplier to 30 percent of the overall consumption.[55] Moreover, Russia has been interested in advanced technologies and financing. All in all, the EU-Russian energy dialogue has so far been successfully used by Russia to 'monopolise' its position as a strategic energy supplier, as the EU gave up two important principles of diversification by accepting the Russian demand for the maintenance of long-term contracts and the absence of quantitative restrictions on fossil fuel imports. This was later extended to the new member states in the Joint Statement on EU enlargement.[56]

Without doubt, the EU-Russia Energy Dialogue has been important for the managing of the energy trade and for addressing the different dimensions related to it. But so far the Energy Dialogue has rather brought more tactical results on day-to-day issues than on strategic questions concerning the building up of an energy space. In some issues - as market harmonisation and market transparency - the strategies fall apart. The relationship is fraught with differences concerning legal norms and ordering principles. Moreover, its start was already flawed with shortcomings in scope. The Energy Dialogue is conducted bilaterally and limited to the EU and Russia. Other countries, which geographically and physically represent part of the market, are not included

54 EU-Russia Energy Dialogue, Second Progress Report, Brussels/ Moscow, May 2002, p.2.

55 EU-Russia Energy Dialogue, Third Progress Report, Brussels/ Moscow, November 2002, p.2.

56 EU-Russia Energy Dialogue, Fifth Progress Report, Brussels/ Moscow, November 2004, p.2.

(such as first and foremost the transit countries). This is even more important because of the fact that one attempt towards including these countries failed mainly because of the Russian position: the Energy Charter Treaty.

7 THE ENERGY CHARTER TREATY

A first attempt towards creating a single energy space - started by a Dutch initiative - was the Energy Charter that was also backed by the EU. The so-called Energy Charter was an early approach in 1990, which mirrored the euphoria at the end of the bipolar world and translated Gorbachev's idea(l) of a common European House into the idea of a common European energy market. The European Union's integration and the need to define a new governance structure for the Single European Market together with new possibilities in the East created the atmosphere in which the idea of an integrated energy market from the East to the West surged. The 1991 European Energy Charter, a not legally binding political commitment for East-West energy cooperation, was proposed by the then Dutch Prime Minister, Ruud Lubbers at the European Council in Dublin in June 1990 as the predecessor of the Energy Charter Treaty. It was the first economic agreement uniting 52 members of the former Soviet Union, the former centrally planned Central and Eastern European states, the EU and Japan, Australia, Norway, Turkey and Switzerland. Important observers were China and Saudi Arabia.

The Energy Charter Treaty, signed in 1994, entered into force as binding and effective under public international law on 16 April 1998. This comprehensive multilateral treaty covers all important areas of energy cooperation such as trade, investment, transit, dispute settlement but also energy efficiency. The Energy Charter Treaty reflects a multilateral governance approach to promote the openness of energy markets and energy security with both the supply security for the consumer and the demand security for the supplier, especially achieved through the non-discriminatory rules for investment and transit. It promotes these goals under the principles of sovereignty over natural resources and sustainable development.[57] The Energy Charter Treaty has been designed as an important instrument for an increase of cooperation in the energy sector and for providing a basis for the creation of an open international energy market under GATT and WTO principles, designed to create an open and transparent international energy market. Apart from building-up an energy community, its main objectives are to set standards for the energy market economy, to provide a basis for contractual and trade relations, and to create a basis for a rule of law.

57 Energy Charter Secretary, The Energy Charter Treaty: A Reader's Guide (Online Version on www.encharter.org), p.7.

The main obstacle for the full application of the Energy Charter Treaty is the Protocol on Transit which indeed is a centrepiece of the treaty. Russia has not ratified the treaty yet and there are no hints that it will ratify it in the near future. This is due to the transit protocol. The treaty with the Transit Protocol would obligate Russia to implement the principles of freedom of transit without distinction of the origin, destination or ownership of the energy, and of non-discriminatory pricing. This has not been perceived as being in the interest of Russia as will be described below. The Russian position has been very strict on the transit issue and this brings up some general questions about Russia's attitude and acceptance of multilateral and legally binding treaties - something that also has implications for EU-Russian relations. The Energy Charter Treaty would transfer WTO rules to the energy trade and thus set regulations and standards for a liberalised, transparent and non-discriminatory energy market.[58] However, it is important to mention that the Energy Charter Treaty was created as an international regime for liberalised trade, investment and transit but that it does not impose privatisation in the energy sector or - even more important - Third Party Access to pipeline networks on the national level. It also reaffirms national sovereignty over energy resources, respectively the right of national governments to determine the territory to be exploited, depletion and reservoir policies and taxation, and the right to participate in exploration and production.

The Energy Charter Treaty can be seen as the most important initiative to govern international energy trade multilaterally and it has been backed by the EU for a long time in order to create a common energy space. On the one hand it is an attempt to achieve equally and fairly applicable and legally binding rules and on the other hand to institutionally integrate many countries of the common neighbourhood into a common space. Thus it is problematic that the EU's main supplier of energy and so-called strategic partner is blocking the Treaty. Moreover, energy policies are seen as a centrepiece of the EU-Russian relationship and the creation of common spaces and this article strongly supports this view.

In order to gain more insight into the energy partnership but also into the prospects of the strategic partnership we will turn to Russian energy policies towards the EU and later on to energy politics within the EU and its member states. This is important because there are three trends apparent in the energy relations. The less probable trend is that the relations will develop on the basis of the Energy Charter Treaty, which is the most integrative and inclusive approach (also in relation to the neighbourhood). Even the future strategic meaning of the EU-Russia Energy Dialogue is not yet clearly defined and manifested because there are bilateral (in the sense of Russian-EU member states) initiatives that might in future undermine and even contradict the

58 Götz, Roland, Die russische Energiewirtschaft und die Energieversorgung Europas, in: Gorzka/ Schulze, Wohin steuert Russland unter Putin?, p.95/96.

common EU-Russian approach if no further measures are undertaken by those member states.

8 RUSSIAN ENERGY POLICY

From the beginning, Russia fought to maintain its pole position as a main energy supplier and a main transit country to Europe. In doing so, Russia anticipated a possible struggle for market shares on the European gas market with Central Asian states. In this struggle Russia has enjoyed a very favourable position in the area of energy transit from the prosperous Caspian and Central Asian region, despite its own dependence as a net purchaser of energy transit in the neighbouring countries, such as Belarus, Ukraine, Poland and the Czech Republic. All possible existing export pipelines from the region run through Russian territory, which made the newly independent states highly dependent on Russia's 'good will' to permit them access to the pipeline network. In order to sell Central Asian gas on the European market, Central Asian gas producers depend on the Russian gas transport infrastructure, which belongs to the big Russian gas monopolist, *Gazprom*. This is where the Energy Charter Treaty comes back in: A ratification of the Energy Charter Treaty might bring claims through the back door to liberalise the Russian gas market and to impose a freer trade regime. The question of the liberalisation of Russia's gas market and consequently the splitting up of *Gazprom's* monopoly into production, transport, supply and export has always been an issue in EU-Russian negotiations about the Energy Charter Treaty, the WTO accession and most recently about the four common spaces.[59] At the same time it does not have any advantage for *Gazprom* or Russia's energy policy. Taking the role of the gas monopolist away this would also have implications for Russia's foreign policy and foreign trade policy as it would deprive the state of a foreign policy weapon for a possible use.

Relying on the monopolist *Gazprom* has paid off for the ruling elite of Russia. Under the Yeltsin administration *Gazprom* had already been an important foreign policy tool. The instrumentalisation of energy dependence for purposes of Russian foreign policy was especially obvious during the Russian-Ukrainian negotiations on the Black Sea fleet in the

59 See: Road Map for the Common Economic Space – Building Blocks for Sustained Economic Growth, p. 16. http://www.europa.eu.int/comm/external_relations/russia/summit_05_05/index.htm (Download 05/11/05).

early 1990s.[60] *Gazprom* had been an important instrument for the Russian government that built its reintegration course on the dependence of the other CIS members on Russian energy supplies and thus had instrumentalized *Gazprom*'s deliveries by turning the gas tap on and off.[61] This created a situation of mutual benefits for the company and the government. Moreover, many connections and personal links existed between the political and the gas elite, as *Gazprom* had been the *alma mater* for many Russian politicians such as the former prime minister Victor Chernomyrdin. *Gazprom* in turn had used the Russian government as an instrument for its own policies, especially because the policy of reintegration included the perspective of low transit costs and easily obtained property rights in the CIS countries.[62] This 'foreign policy free-lancing' was soon reversed by Putin through 'incorporation': Putin established a tighter control over the gas monopolist by appointing his close ally from Petersburg, Aleksej Miller, to the post of chief executive in 2001.[63] This also had consequences for the corporate governance and strategies.

The former *Gazprom* chief executive, Vyakhirev, had built upon the existing long-term contracts with - among others - *Ruhrgas* and *Gaz de France*, as well as on a strong, even monopolist position of *Gazprom* as a supplier to the European market. This well-targeted 'downstream-headed' strategy was accompanied by a calculated entrance into other markets. [64] This was possible because *Gazprom* controlled and operated the Russian natural gas grid. This is the reason why the principle of reciprocity (introduced by the Energy Charter Treaty) is not seen as favourable for *Gazprom* and for Russia's foreign (economic) policies.

The new CEO Miller reinforced the dependency of the Central Asian gas producers. *Gazprom* along with Putin's policy de facto realised the so-called 'Gas-OPEC' by using Russia's good bargaining position. All major pipelines from Central Asian gas fields are

60 See Sahm, Astrid / Westphal, Kirsten, Power and the Yamal Pipeline, in: Balmaceda, Margarita M./ Clem, James I./ Tarlow, Lisbeth, Independent Belarus, Domestic Determinants, Regional Dynamics, and Implications for the West, Cambridge, 2002, pp.270-301.

61 Westphal, Kirsten , Hegemon statt Partner - Rußlands Politik gegenüber dem "nahen Ausland" (Münster 1995); Pappe, Yakov, Neftyanaya i gazovaya diplomatiya Rossii, Pro et Contra Vol. 2 (1997), No. 3, pp. 55-71.

62 See Krjukov, Valery/ Moe, Arild ,The new Russian Corporation? A Case Study of Gazprom (London 1996), p. 29.

63 Gazprom is organised as a private sector company but with a 38 % share of the government and a very special relationship with the government, as the 38 % state share is normally exercised together with the company's treasury stock, which makes up 51 %.

64 For more details see: Westphal, Kirsten, Russische Energiepolitik, Nomos: Baden-Baden, 2000: 98-106

running to and through Russia and therefore the only way to sell a significant amount of gas abroad is, at the moment, to Russia. Russia has used this situation and concluded bilateral treaties with Kazakhstan and Turkmenistan. In 2002, Putin suggested to create a Eurasian gas alliance among the post-Soviet gas producers. So far, the Central Asian output represents about 15 percent of the Russian production.[65] At the moment the imports from Central Asia are not necessarily needed but in the future the long-term contract between Turkmenistan and Russia on gas deliveries will be used to maintain Russia's position as a gas supplier to the European markets. In fact, *Gazprom* sold Central Asian gas to low prices to Russian and former Soviet Union consumers and exported its freed-up surplus for higher prices to European markets and in doing so, gained high windfall profits.

By and large, the connection between the Putin administration and the oil and gas industry has become closer since 2000. Putin has reversed the Yeltsin system of 'foreign policy free-lancing' by 'incorporation'. Yeltsin chose a strategy of privatising and selling assets of the oil industry to appease regional leaders or - after his re-election in 1996 - in order to reward the so-called oligarchs who supported his election campaign. Putin has even stepped backwards, as is shown by the *Yukos* case, and seems to re-nationalise huge parts of the oil industry.[66] It can be assumed that the *Gazprom* example as a state-dominated monopoly and to a lesser extent the example of *Transneft*, the state-dominated oil transport monopoly, have worked as a precedent. Moreover, the price increases of the 2000s have been to the benefit of the Putin government and the revenues have further diminished the dependence on tax payments from the oil companies owned by those oil tycoons who had had a huge political influence under Yeltsin. This has prompted the Russian government to rethink the structure of the energy industry, the contracts and the system of royalties and taxes.[67] In the case of *Yukos* the political and economic interests fell together. *Yukos* chief Khodorkovsky openly questioned and undermined Putin's energy policy with his

65 Rontoyanni, Clelia, Russia and the CIS: Energy and International Relations, Paper presented at the ISA Convention, 26-28 June 2003, Budapest.

66 The owner of *YUKOS*, one of the so-called oligarchs, Mikhail Khodorkowsky, not only expanded the company's economic weight but also increasingly exerted political influence by financing opposition parties. *YUKOS* also had plans for oil deliveries to China and for a pipeline project to China that would have countered the transport monopoly of *Transneft*. In many points *YUKOS* and Khodorkowsky were thus in opposition to Putin's politics. Khodorkowsky was put in jail in 2003 and accused of tax evasion and offences in the privatization process. By using a letterbox company, the main production site of *YUKOS*, *Yuganskneftegaz*, was sold to *Rosneft*, the Russian state oil company, after Gazprom had withdrawn, fearing disadvantages because of judicial steps undertaken by *YUKOS* in the US.

67 'Oil companies in quandary over cash glut', in: IHT, 02/12-13/2005.

plans to open the company for huge foreign investment by the planned merger between *Yukos* and *Sibneft* and his plans to build a pipeline to China, which would have questioned the state transport monopoly of *Transneft*.

All in all, Putin has consolidated and centralised the political and economic power in his hands over the last five years. There are many signs for that in the energy sector, such as the discussion to raise the state's share in *Gazprom* from 38 percent to over 50 percent[68] or the fact that *Rosneft*, the state oil company, has bought the former *Yukos* core producing subsidiary, *Yuganskneftegas*, or the splitting up of *Yukos*, as well as the Khodorkovsky case itself. Another sign for the increased state influence is the Russian energy strategy of 2003.[69] On some occasions foreign investment and activities were revised and the planned law on natural resources is also seen as keeping foreign investors out of so-called strategic production sites.[70] At the moment of a growing competition among energy consuming countries which all focus on Russia as the main producer outside the OPEC, Putin seems to consequently consolidate 'his hold' on the main assets of the oil and gas industry. In terms of the EU-Russia Energy Dialogue with its two objectives of market harmonisation and *constructive* interdependence based on and framed by a stable and transparent set of institutions, this is a clear step backwards. Together with the 'failure' of the Energy Charter Treaty this has to be perceived as an alarm signal by the EU.

9 EU ENERGY POLICIES

The EU has so far "put all eggs into the Russian basket"[71], a fact that is only logical and comprehensible up to a certain point, as the two regions have longstanding energy trade relations, as Russia is in possession of around 30 percent of the world's gas reserves and as it is an important alternative oil supplier to the world market, thereby balancing OPEC's influence. Given the fact, however, that the Western Siberian reserves are already exploited to more than 60 per cent and exploration, production

68 Süddeutsche Zeitung, 05/19/05, p.28.

69 See. Götz, Roland, Die russische Energiewirtschaft, p.88-90.

70 So far the Subsoil Law is still under discussion, see: Deputaty Gosudarstvennoy Dumy RF 3 avgusta 2004 g. prinyali vo vtorom chtenii zakonoproekt o vnesenii izmenii v ryad zakonodatelnykh aktov RF, vklyuchayushchikh popravki k zakonu ‚O nedrakh', http://www.oil-industry.ru/newsdetail.asp?id=2233&template=1 (Download 08/04/04)

71 Peters, Susanne, Building-Up the potential for future resource Conflicts: The Shortcomings of Western Response Strategies to New Energy Vulnerabilities, RSC No. 2003/9 Transatlantic Programme Series, p.20.

and transport prices will increase with the tapping of new reserves in the Far East and North, it would be more consequent from an economic point of view to look for fuels which are geographically closer and cheaper, such as Central Asian and Caspian oil and gas. Moreover, Russian reorientation towards the US and the East puts Europe's plans in danger. The gas produced on the Yamal peninsula and in the Barents Sea could also be transformed into liquefied natural gas and be sold to the US and Asia at some point in the future. The new rounds of EU enlargement with Bulgaria and Rumania (and later possibly Turkey) will bring the Caspian region closer to the European Union's borders. It would be consequent to look for closer economic ties with the Central Asian and Caspian region. Last but not least, with the construction of the so-called Baku-Tbilissi-Ceyhan oil pipeline and the planned Baku-Erzurum gas pipeline Turkey is already on its way to become an important energy corridor to Europe. Turkey would also function as an energy bridge between the EU and Iran.

Energy policy in the EU has only slowly started to pay attention to the management of its external energy supplies. One reason for the delay is that the EU has not pooled competencies in the energy policy, despite the fact that the European integration process did always have an energy political dimension with Euratom and the European Community of Coal and Steel, which ended in July 2002. Energy issues in the European Union are still mainly treated on a national level.[72] Explicitly, any attempts to include a chapter of energy into the treaties of Rome, Maastricht and Amsterdam have failed. Therefore, energy policy has only been conducted indirectly by other common policies as transport, environment and the single market. The so-called Green Paper of 2000 clearly states that the EU has very limited scope to influence energy supply conditions.

The European Commission's Green Paper[73] tried to start a debate on the security of energy supply in Europe as energy import dependency is expected to increase because of a rise in the demand for energy, the changes in the energy mix and decreased production of primary energy in the EU. However, the Green Paper also mainly focuses on the demand side in order to reduce the risks of energy supply dependency, and explicitly makes energy saving a key to its intervention to reduce the risk of energy dependence. The three priorities of European energy policy are environmental and climate policy, the single European market, and the security of energy supply. The EU politics put a clear emphasis on environmental and climate policies, as well as on the internal market. EU energy policies have been focusing on

72 For a detailed description of EU energy policies: Westphal, Kirsten , Handlungsbedarf. Die Energiepolitik der Europäischen Union, in: Europa unter Spannung, Energiepolitik zwischen Ost und West, Osteuropa 9-10, 2004, pp. 39-54.

73 Commission of the European Communities, Green Paper – Towards a European Strategy for the security of energy supply, COM (2000) 769 final, November 2000.

the creation of the internal market. In 1997 and 1998, the EU has successfully started to liberalise their gas and electricity markets. The markets will be fully liberalised by 2005, private households by 2007. Moreover, the EU strongly promoted the Kyoto Protocol and committed itself to the reduction of its greenhouse gas emissions by eight percent below the 1990 level.

The European constitution does for the first time foresee a shared competence between the member states and the union. Whether this will be put through if the constitution itself is approved has yet to be proved. As mentioned above, the EU so far has no competencies in the energy policy. This is an explanation for the short-comings in the forming of external energy relations, especially in the face of the demand for diversification. The strong argument that a domestic management within the common internal market requires a common approach can be extended and has to be emphasised even more in the external dimension of managing energy dependency. In Brussels there is a slowly growing consciousness that managing external energy dependency is also a security and foreign policy issue. Despite the creation of an internal market and the common commitment to sustainability, coming to a common energy policy has been so difficult because of the diverse situations in the member states. The EU is composed of energy-rich states such as the UK and the Netherlands, which are characterised by a high consciousness towards energy issues but which are at the same time reluctant to pool sovereignty in that field. Other member states have hardly any resources. Others again possess big and powerful energy companies such as France where *TotalFinaElf* and its predecessors have played an instrumental role in foreign policy. Member states-based companies such as the German company *Ruhrgas* enjoy a favourable and privileged position in Russia.

For Germany, it is not yet clear whether it seeks to take advantage of a 'special' relationship with Russia that also build on a strong personal relationship between Putin and the German Chancellor Schröder. Turning a blind eye to Putin's step backwards with regard to democracy, the human rights and the media policy has led to harsh criticism of Schröder's policy that has been accused of trading 'silence for gas'.[74] This interpretation implies a strategic German interest. First and foremost because of Russian oil and natural gas deliveries and secondly because of the Russian market as a field of activity for German enterprises. Putin and Schröder also personally supported

[74] Götz, Roland, Schweigen für Gas? Deutschlands Abhängigkeit von Rußlands Energielieferungen, in: SWP aktuell Nr. 43, September 2004.

the last *Wintershall* & *Gazprom* deal[75] of April 2005 to build a pipeline through the Baltic Sea from Vyborg to Greifswald. For Schröder, this is a clear support of the German energy sector in order to fix its exclusive and privileged position in Russia. For Putin, this deal means a lot with regard to more autonomy and independence from transit countries and thus leverage for his foreign policy towards the transit countries of Belarus and Ukraine in particular.[76] Under these terms the German strategy to build on bilateral relations and exclusive access in its energy relations with Russia undermines the multilateral EU approach to a certain extent. Therefore, it first of all has to again be interlaced with EU initiatives, and secondly, it has to be directed at also integrating the neighbouring countries into its policies. German policy has to consider that and work for an integrative approach to maintain diversified pipeline routes and to support a Ukrainian position as a main transit country to the EU as one means of 'building a common space'. What is needed is a clear political signal to the Eastern European countries that the Baltic pipeline project will not question or erode their position as transit countries. These efforts have to be paralleled by a joint EU initiative to further promote a market harmonisation and common ordering principles. This might be even more effectively done on the level of the Energy Charter process than on the EU-Russian energy dialogue level, as the Energy Charter process builds on multilateralism which includes all parties involved.

However, the mosaic of interests and economic and political calculations described above has made it difficult to find a common approach, and has complicated existing approaches.

75 *Gazprom* and the German company *Wintershall* made a package deal on jointly developing the *Yuzhno Russkoye* gas field in Western Siberia with *Wintershall*, a *BASF* subsidiary, increasing *Wintershall's* stake to 49 percent. The field could cover Germany's gas consumption for five years. In turn, *Gazprom* will strengthen its presence as a gas trading and selling company in Europe. *Gazprom* will rise its stake in *Wingas*, a joint venture established in 1993, from 35 percent to 49 percent. The major project the two companies announced to get started by the end of 2005 is the Baltic gas pipeline. This gas pipeline will run from Vyborg through the Baltic Sea to Greifswald in Germany. The ambitious project that will cost between $8 to $10 billion, is extremely important to *Gazprom*. See: International Herald Tribune, 12/04/05, p.4.

76 On transit questions in Ukraine see: Balmaceda, Margarita, Ukraine's Energy Policy and U.S. Strategic Interests in Eurasia, in: Woodrow Wilson, International Center for Scholars Kennan Institute, Occasional Paper #291, 2004.

10 THE ENERGY FACTOR IN EU-RUSSIAN RELATIONS

When turning to the 'energy factor' in the partnership it is important to mention the structural characteristics of energy relations: To build up energy relations is a long-term issue, as the energy infrastructure is highly cost-intensive and not very flexible. Transportation structures and facilities establish connections between countries and between regions over a long time.[77] At best, these connections are interpreted and perceived as an *interdependence* by both, the consumer and supplier, a perception that then lays the basis for a cooperative relationship. There are some aspects of (inter)dependence to be mentioned because they can transform into risks[78] if not managed positively to serve both the consuming and producing countries.

The trade in fossil fuels creates 1) *physical (inter)dependence* that is conditioned by the existing infrastructure; with the risk of disruptions; 2) *economic (inter)dependence*, as the consumer states are interested in a stable supply of energy while supplier states are interested in selling their energy sources; 3) *social (inter)dependence*, because energy prices highly affect the wealth distribution, and the volatility of oil and gas prices has effects on growth and therefore bears risks for the socio-economic development; 4) *political (inter)dependence*, as at best there is a mutual dependency that forces to cooperate, but energy trade also contains a high risk of structural dependence that opens the opportunity to political pressure and to use the 'oil (or gas) weapon' in order to enforce ones own will; and 5) *ecological (inter)dependence*, as the production, transportation and consumption of energy highly affects the environment regardless of national borders with the risks of environmental damage and climate change.

The EU-Russia Energy Dialogue and the Energy Charter Treaty have tried to balance these risks and aim for a steady and affordable flow of oil, gas and electricity in sufficient quantities. Yet, the Energy Charter Treaty has not worked sufficiently because of the Russian blockade of the transit protocol. The Energy Dialogue is hence more limited to day-to-day business than to the solution of basic questions and to arriving at substantial institutional settings. First, the development of the EU-Russian energy relationship displays the lack of a multilateral framework which provides transparency and legal certainty. Secondly and in consequence of the former, the EU-Russian energy dialogue does not sufficiently integrate the 'common neighbourhood' into the conception and construction of an 'energy space'. Thirdly, de facto both partners follow a 'pick and choose' strategy. Although the Commission as the

77 This is not only the fact for gas but also for oil. Physically, the oil flows are exceedingly determined by infrastructure and chemical characteristics, while the oil market is only virtually global through the price setting mechanisms on the stock exchanges.

78 For risks see: European Commission, Greenpaper, Towards a European strategy for the security of energy supply, (COM(2000) 769 final).

conductor of the dialogue from the EU side follows the strategy of negotiating a 'package deal', some of the member states follow their own agendas parallel to that.

To sum up, the EU-Russian energy relationship is mainly moderated by the Energy Dialogue which addresses the issues of physical and ecological risks and by the interdependencies caused. This way infrastructure projects are promoted and the Kyoto protocol has entered into force. The latter is also important because it includes a crucial multilateral treaty on a global level that has been supported by the EU over a long time and finally found support by Russia last year - a support that has been crucial for its entering into force. However, the socio-economic and political risks are mediated in reliance on personal relationships and along short-term issues but without so far providing a substantial and reliable institutional set and legal framework for a functioning market order. The market principle, competition and liberalisation of energy markets are aimed to balance price increases and the interplay between supply and demand, and are thus seen as a contribution to diversification (of different sources, countries of origin and a diversity of actors). Diversification is a key to energy security. So far, Russia has abstained from making a clear commitment to this ordering principle which would mediate and balance these economic risks which are closely related to social and political risks. Political risks such as encountering external pressure can also be limited by a diversity of state, public-private and private actors which are engaged in the energy trade.

There are numerous rifts in the EU-Russian energy relationship that touch upon state and market functions. One key difference is to what extent "*states* or *markets* are seen as the main device for coordinating industrial - and state-behaviour"[79] in order to manage energy supply and demand security. Another difference is the degree of *institutional* integration in a given region and possible spill-over effects into other areas of policy. The vital, strategic and indispensable role energy sources play in any economy makes energy a particular and special good that demands a strong role played by the state in the regulation of energy trade. However, market relations and an integrative market balance the above mentioned risks related to energy trade under a clear, transparent and stable framework instead of subjecting them to state dominance. In order to achieve this integrated market 'space', it is pivotal to understand that energy trade creates *inter*dependence. This makes a universal definition of energy as a commercial good and a service (for transport and distribution) inevitable. The question is whether interdependence is managed along anonymously and equally applied rules. This is the precondition for a common and open space that is created constructively and is based on positive interdependence. It is not by chance that chapter 4 of the common economic space on energy highlights as actions "the convergence of EU and

79 Clingendael International Energy Programme: Study on Energy Supply Security and Geopolitics, Final Report prepared for DG TREN, The Hague, January 2004, p.85.

Russian energy strategies" and "the integration of electricity markets, including ensuring a level playing field in terms of equivalent basic rules (...)".[80]

Even though energy is a centrepiece and a factor to drive the relations further it is also a field that has revealed the difficulties arising while trying to deepen the relations. Energy relations also suffer from the 'value gap' in the sense that it makes evident two different approaches, one of a power and state-control-based approach, the other one rather based on the market and institutions that build on transparency, reliability and legal certainty. The two approaches are contradictory as they refer to differing logics and ordering principles. Moreover, Russia relies on exclusiveness and on a 'pick and choose' behaviour, and that makes it difficult to pursue the creation of a common space. However, a common space includes and encompasses *per definitionem* the common neighbourhood.

The EU and Russia have defined energy as a primary cooperation basis because it establishes steady and long-term relations. The EU-Russian approach has been prudent to include the energy relations into the creation of the economic space and not to define a separate field of activity, also in order to achieve spill-over and trade-off effects. The fact that the EU and Russia have so far not achieved significant progress in an institutional and legal framework in their Energy Dialogue in this central area is on the one hand symptomatic for the overall relationship. But on the other hand it also reflects that energy relations are a special field because of the particularities of energy. Thus the energy partnership is a real testing ground as it combines all of the controversial issues with regard to multilateral cooperation and order, to the common neighbourhood, and the role of the state in economy and society. Energy companies, post-Soviet infrastructure and energy abundance in general have been one of the few remaining powerful and effective foreign policy instrument of Russia, both to structure the post-Soviet space and relationships with the newly independent states, as well as to integrate itself into the global market. Besides, cheap energy was one of the means to cushion the economic transformation.

Energy relations are a tricky testing ground because of the particularities of energy. Even in the EU, energy has proved to be a sensitive political area and one of the last sectors in which the domestic market has been liberalised in the EU, because even member states fear interferences from Brussels and have been reluctant to pool sovereignty. Moreover, the energy markets demand a re-regulation and a stable and transparent framework set by the state because of the socio-economic impact that energy prices and availability have on the whole economy. This is even more true in the case of Russia. Thus it has been the right strategy that energy has been included into the common economic space as it can be expected that market harmonisation and legal framework setting might take place sooner in other areas than in - for instance -

80 See: Road Map for the Common Economic Space, p. 16.

the gas sector. Market harmonisation and market rules are also highly asymmetrical issues as the EU by and large sets the conditions and places the burden of transformation on Russia. Nevertheless and even by taking this argument into account, what is problematic and heavily interferes with the overall relationship are significant steps backward. As such, the *Yukos* affair as the most prominent example for the process of re-concentration or even the incorporation of Russian energy companies are serious impediments for the 'four common spaces'.

This does not *per se* question the security of Russian energy supply to Europe but wants to stress that there is still a long way to go on the road to establishing a common energy space and that the 'going gets tough' also because EU member states are lacking unity. However, there is also still a long way to go in international relations to see energy as a commercial and not as a strategic good. Taking this into account, the EU-Russian Energy Dialogue and a common energy space is not only an important and strategic project from a regional but also from a global point of view, as is its inclusive and integrative character.

11 CONCLUSIONS

The analysis has shown that the EU-Russian relationship has been formulated as an encompassing partnership with the objective to establish a common space for security and stability in Europe. This approach reflects the special role of Russia as the biggest neighbour and an (at least geographically) integral part of Europe.

Two conclusions can be drawn: 1) Form is still prevailing over substance, and 2) the partnership is driven by economic interests and in particular by energy deliveries. The economic interests of both partners play an important role and are a driving factor for the relations. The EU has a pronounced interest in energy deliveries, but also in Russia itself as a market and a field for investments. For Russia the EU is the major trading partner and the bulk of FDI comes from the EU. Russia is also pivotal in questions of stability and security in Europe, not only because of its sheer size. Therefore, the EU and Russia have agreed on four road maps for common spaces. What has become apparent is a clear prevalence of form over substance. The partnership has produced numerous documents, declarations and has established many working groups and committees, but when it comes to concrete decisions and substantial definitions concerning setting and implementation, a 'value gap' is evident. Russia has ordering principles such as 'top-down governance' in a 'managed democracy', a selective application of law and state dominance in strategic economic sectors that diverge from and contradict the EU multi-level governance approach based on market principle, the rule of law and democratic governance. This will at best create 'a bumpy road' for the implementation of the road maps for the common spaces. It might also lead to nowhere. Of course, the EU consistently follows the approved pattern of expanding its space of economic activity and common rules and regulations to Russia. And, of course, this creates an asymmetry in the relations as the EU is imposing its standards, rules and norms which makes it more difficult for Russia to accept and to reach compliance. But for Russia it is not just a question of reluctance to 'take over' EU norms, but Russia also refrains from certain principles such as an equitable appliance of law that is a basis for common spaces. It even takes steps backwards in democratic and market governance.

Another factor is that the coherence of the EU approach towards Russia has eroded. The EU's policy towards Russia is especially and more and more defined by the new member states, which are increasingly sensitive to Russia's policy towards the 'near abroad'. On the other hand, 'old' member states such as Germany emphasise the special relationship with Russia. The EU is stipulated to think over its concept of a 'Wider Europe' and the European Neighbourhood Policy under the aspect of the role Russia will have to play. So far, the concept is not clear and does not consider the special role and position of Russia. The EU has committed itself to the strategic partnership with Russia but has so far not developed an idea of how to interlace the strategic partnership with the Neighbourhood policy.

The going gets tough and tougher with the approaching end of Putin's second term which will end in 2008. With the signing of the four road maps of the common spaces a window of opportunity has been re-opened. Even though its is just a declaration of intent and the main gaps and conflict issues remain, it still provides 'roads maps' that should be used for 'travelling' together. For that purpose, the EU has to further work on strengthening the political dialogue and cooperation under the principles of human rights, democratic governance, the rule of law and market order. The informal division of labour between the OSCE and the Council of Europe on the one hand and the EU on the other hand in demanding compliance with internationally agreed norms and economic cooperation has to become closer again. The fact that there is more form than substance hints to the fact that the relations have been de-politicised for several reasons. First, the Russian economisation of foreign policy that fell together with a difficult economic situation in Germany, France and other 'old' member states. Secondly, as described for the German case, member states have given priority to economics over politics as well. Third, in order to follow economic interests, the political issues such as the *Yukos* case, the situation in Chechnya, and the election-related issues in Georgia, in Ukraine and Kyrgyzstan have been 'outsourced' and mainly been treated on the level of the OSCE and the Council of Europe. The Ukrainian politics and the 'common neighbourhood' east of the EU and west of Russia have to be integrated again and tackled on the EU level. The politisation that has also taken place in Russian-EU relations with the 'Orange Revolution'[81] can thus be seen as a chance to

[81] I would like to thank Sabine Fischer for some useful comments on that issue.

bring the strategic relationship further. The EU has to take care that the concepts of a 'wider Europe' and a 'wider Russia' do not develop a geopolitical gap in Europe but are developed further towards a common space of democratic stability and sustainable economic growth.

References

Balmaceda, Margarita (2004), Ukraine's Energy Policy and U.S. Strategic Interests in Eurasia, in: Woodrow Wilson, International Center for Scholars Kennan Institute, Occasional Paper #291

Birckenbach, Hanne-Margret/ Wellmann Christian (eds.) (2003), The Kaliningrad Challenge. Options and Recommendations, Münster

Birckenbach, Hanne-Margret (2003), Für ein europäisches Haus in Kaliningrad, in: SCHIFF-Texte 72, Dec. 2003

Clingendael International Energy Programme: Study on Energy Supply Security and Geopolitics (2004), Final Report prepared for DG TREN, The Hague, January 2004

Erler, Gernot (2004) Der Fall Chodorkowskij - Zur Tomographie eines politischen Konflikts, in: Gabriele Gorzka/ Peter W Schulze, Wohin steuert Russland unter Putin?, Der autoritäre Weg in die Demokratie, Frankfurt: Campus, 2004, S. 301-325.

Fischer, Sabine (2003), Russlands Westpolitik in der Krise 1992-2000. Eine konstruktivistische Untersuchung, Frankfurt a.M./ New York, 2003.

Fischer, Sabine (2005), Rußland und die Ukraine, Fehlkalkulation oder neoimperialer Impuls?, in: Osteuropa, 55Jg., 1/2005

Götz, Roland (2002), Rußlands Erdgas und die Energiesicherheit der EU, SWP Studie 12/ April 2002

Götz, Roland (2004a) Russlands Energiestrategie und die Energieversorgung Europas, SWP Sudie 6, März 2004

Götz, Roland (2004b), Die russische Energiewirtschaft und die Energieversorgung Europas, in: Gabriele Gorzka/ Peter W Schulze, Wohin steuert Russland unter Putin?, Der autoritäre Weg in die Demokratie, Frankfurt: Campus, 2004, S. 87-115

Götz, Roland (2004c) Schweigen für Gas? Deutschlands Abhängigkeit von Rußlands Energielieferungen, in: SWP aktuell Nr. 43, September 2004

Gorzka G./ Schulze P.-W., Wohin steuert Russland unter Putin?, Der autoritäre Weg in die Demokratie, Frankfurt: Campus, 2004

Kempe, Iris, (2002), Die Europäische Union und Rußland nach dem 11. September, in: Europäische Rundschau, 30. Jhg., 2002/2, p. 107-118

Krjukov, Valerij/ Moe Arild (1996), The new Russian Corporation? A Case Study of Gazprom, London

Meier Christian (2004), Nach dem Gipfel von Den Haag, SWP aktuell 58/ Dez. 2004

Pappe Yakov (1997), Neftyanaya i gazovaya diplomatiya Rossii, Pro et Contra Vol. 2 (1997), No. 3, pp. 55-71

Peters Susanne (2003), Building-Up the Potential for Future Resource Conflicts: The Shortcomings of Western Response Strategies to New Energy Vulnerabilities, RSC No. 2003/9 Transatlantic Programme Series

Pleines Heiko (2004), Der Moskauer EU-Russland Gipfel, in: Russland-Analysen 28/2004, p.2-4.

Rar, Aleksandr (2005), Itogi Gannovera - plokhaya novost' dlya Yushchenko, in: Neftegazovaya Vertikal' - Novostnaya Lenta 12.04.05

Romanova, Tatiana A. (2003), Stanovlenye Evropeyskogo Soyuza kak mezhdunarodnogo aktora (na primere investizionnogo sotrudnichestva ES s Rossiye v energeticheskoy sferye, St. Peterburg: St. Peterburgskogo Universiteta 2003

Romanova, Tatiana (2005), Energy Dialogue from Strategic Partnership to the Regional Level of Northern Dimension, Draft February-March 2005

Rontoyanni, Clelia (2003), Russia and the CIS: Energy and International Relations, Paper presented at the ISA Convention, 26-28 June 2003, Budapest

Sahm Astrid/ Westphal Kirsten (2002), Power and the Yamal Pipeline, in: Balmaceda, Margarita M./ Clem, James I./ Tarlow, Lisbeth, Independent Belarus, Domestic Determinants, Regional Dynamics, and Implications for the West, Cambridge, pp.270-301

Shevtsova Lilia (2003), Putin's Russia, Carnegie Endowment for International Peace: Washington D.C.

Victor, David G./ Victor, Nadejda M. (2003), Axis of Oil?, in: Foreign Affairs vol. 82, No. 2, March/ April 2003, p.47-61

Westphal Kirsten (1995), Hegemon statt Partner - Rußlands Politik gegenüber dem "nahen Ausland", Münster

Westphal, Kirsten (2000), Russische Energiepolitik, Nomos: Baden-Baden

Westphal Kirsten (2004), Handlungsbedarf. Die Energiepolitik der Europäischen Union, in: Europa unter Spannung, Energiepolitik zwischen Ost und West, Osteuropa 9-10, 2004, pp. 39-54

Zagorski Andrei (2004), Putins zweite Amtszeit, in: Russland-Analysen 48/04, p.2-5

Documents

Commission of the European Communities, Green Paper - Towards a European Strategy for the security of energy supply, COM (200) 769 final, November 2000

EC, Communication from the Commission to the Council and the European Parliament on relations with Russia, COM (2004) 106, Download 09/02/04

EC, Commission of the EC, Green Paper - Towards an European Strategy for the security of energy supply, COM (2000)769final, Brussels, November 2000

EC Communication (2004) 777 final, The Energy Dialogue between the European Union and the Russian Federation between 2000 and 2004, Brussels 13.12.2004.

Country Strategy Paper 2002-2006, National Indicative Programme 2003-2003, Russian Federation, http://www.europa.eu.int/comm/external_relations/ceeca/com_strat/russia_99.pdf (Download 04/29/2005)

European Neighbourhood Policy Communication COM(2004) 373 final, Brussels, May 2004

Russia's Middle Term Strategy towards the EU (2000-2010), http://www.delrus.cec.eu.int/en/p_245.htm (Download 04/29/05)

Energy Charter Secretary, The Energy Charter Treaty: A Reader's Guide (Online Version on www.encharter.org)

Deputaty Gosudarstvennoy Dumy RF 3 avgusta 2004 g. prinyali vo vtorom chtenii zakonoproekt o vnesenii izmenii v ryad zakonodatelnykh aktov RF, vklyuchayushchikh popravki k zakonu ‚O nedrakh', http://www.oil-industry.ru/newsdetail.asp?id=2233&template=1 (Download 08/04/04)

EU-Russia Agreement on Partnership and Cooperation http://www.europa.eu.int/comm/external_relations/ceeca/pca/pca_russia.pdf (Download 04/29/2005)

EU Common Strategy on Russia http://www.europa.eu.int/comm/external_relations/ceeca/com_strat/index.htm (Download 04/29/2005)

EU-Russian Agreement on the Roads Maps for Common Spaces http://www.europa.eu.int/comm/external_relations/russia/summit_05_05/index.htm (Download 05/11/05).

Progress Reports of the Energy Dialogue: http://www.europa.eu.int/comm/energy/russia/overview/index_en.htm

LA TRANSFORMATION STRUCTURELLE DE L'UE ET LA REDEFINITION POLITIQUE DE L'EUROPE

PIERRE BAILLY

1 INTRODUCTION

L'Union européenne n'apparaît pas comme un acteur global, la faiblesse des dimensions politiques et militaires le lui interdit, malgré l'importance de cet ensemble économique au sein duquel seul le marché est unifié. Les autres dimensions de l'économie (monnaie, protection sociale, place des services non marchands...) ne font pas l'objet d'harmonisation ; la régulation de l'ensemble reste à construire

Envisager la place de l'UE au sein de la géopolitique mondiale nécessite le choix dune hypothèse sur la structure envisageable de l'économie mondiale. Au plan de l'économie politique internationale, il est possible de repérer trois manières de percevoir les acteurs structurant les relations internationales. La première, la plus usuelle, consiste à donner la priorité aux États qui resteraient les acteurs principaux, la seconde à raisonner en termes de mondialisation, la troisième est de reconnaître l'existence de régions.

Ces trois approches sont souvent considérées comme alternatives. En fait ces trois niveaux de réalités qui sont emboîtées et le sont depuis longtemps, les États restent incontournables néanmoins ils choisissent de développer des structures régionales. Il ne semble pas y avoir de structuration économique régionale spontanée. La mise en valeur des capitaux est fondamentalement indifférente aux structures politiques, elle s'adapte aux contraintes imposées par ces structures. Les constructions régionales sont multiples, seules quelques-unes ont une véritable existence, d'autres sont formelles et beaucoup ont disparu. Les structures régionales sont souvent polarisées par un État dominant (ALENA, MERCOSUR, SACD, CEI) qui joue un rôle dirigeant. L'Union européenne constitue une exception car sa construction repose fondamentalement sur l'égalité entre les États membres. Cette construction atypique est durable. Les régions restent encore des réalités floues dans le contexte international, leur place au sein de la configuration internationale est problématique. Le positionnement de l'Union européenne au sein des relations internationales s'est transformé. Durant toute une période de constitution, la Communauté européenne ne s'est pas positionnée dans un cadre international, c'est sous la pression des événements que la question de la place internationale de l'UE s'est trouvée posée.

2 UNE ABSENCE DE POLITIQUE INTERNATIONALE

La mise en œuvre de la CEE se réalise dans un contexte peu favorable pour les États de l'Europe occidentale. L'année 1956 a démontré aux plus puissants d'entre eux qu'ils ne pouvaient plus avoir une politique internationale autonome. L'expédition de Suez est suspendue du fait du double veto des États-Unis et de l'URSS, la crise hongroise illustre l'impuissance des Etats européens devant l'accord des deux superpuissances.

Il est clair que l'Europe n'a pas retrouvé sa capacité politique et militaire entre autres du fait de son retard économique vis-à-vis des États-Unis. Le choix de l'économique est un moyen de retrouver une capacité d'influer sur les événements mondiaux. Dans un premier temps, les institutions communautaires ont pour objectif principal de se renforcer dans une logique de construction d'un marché commun permettant aux États membres de reconstruire leur puissance. Du point vue politique et militaire la CEE est intégrée au camp occidental et bénéficie de la protection apportée par l'OTAN, du point de vue économique les économies nationales prospèrent en développant les ouvertures économiques internationales. La CEE représente dans les années 1960 une des formes de construction d'une unification européenne, d'autres propositions, d'autres projets sont en concurrence : Conseil de l'Europe, AELE etc. Le processus d'intégration généré par la CEE se révèle plus attractif et plus efficace qu'une simple zone de libre-échange comme l'AELE. La CEE fournit les avantages d'une zone de libre-échange (sans implication des États dans les champs militaires et diplomatiques) et assure la régulation des relations entre les États membres au sein des institutions communautaires. L'UE émergera comme l'institution la plus à même de s'adapter et de se développer. Elle finira par absorber ou inféoder les organisations concurrentes de l'UEO à une partie du CAEM.

2.1 Une première phase au sein du bloc occidental

La CECA puis la CEE se sont construites et développées d'abord en fonction de préoccupations politiques (assurer la paix) sous pression des Etats-Unis (obligation de coopération OECE, aide Marshall) puis d'alliance avec ceux-ci dans le contexte de la confrontation avec l'URSS. La première Europe des années 1960-1970 est d'abord une coopération entre États qui trouve dans cette institution un moyen de trouver ou retrouver une plus grande puissance tant politique qu'économique. Il s'agit de renforcer les États par le biais d'une confédération avec institution du droit de veto pour chaque État. Le tarif extérieur commun est l'emblème de cette zone de libre-échange. La PAC représente la politique dominante et vise à transformer l'activité agricole traditionnelle en une activité moderne et productive en assurant une transition pas trop brutale. Les projets par trop fédéralistes échouent régulièrement, c'est le cas emblématique de la CED. La construction politique directe se révélant impraticable, le détour économique a paru plus efficace pour développer ultérieurement une Europe fédérale. Dans une phase d'élaboration d'un marché commun, il n'est nul besoin d'une représentation unique des participants à l'exception des négociations commerciales internationales.

2.2 Une seconde phase de bouleversement

À partir des années 1970, la CEE se trouve dans une phase difficile qui durera jusqu'à la fin des années 1980. Durant cette période, la CEE se révèle attractive avec l'extension des États membres et l'influence qu'elle exerce sur les États voisins et sur une partie de ce qu'on appelle encore le Tiers-Monde. Cette expansion se réalise au sein d'un environnement économique puis politique en mutation profonde. Les relations économiques internationales se modifient radicalement en raison d'un ensemble d'événements.

Au plan monétaire, la décision de suspendre la convertibilité du dollar en 1971 prise par R. Nixon marque la fin aux accords du système monétaire international fondé sur des taux de change fixes mais ajustables. Il laisse la place au flottement généralisé des monnaies. La réponse de la CEE sera de construire un système monétaire européen pour assurer une stabilité des taux de change entre monnaies des États membres. Les avatars des différents systèmes mis en place conduiront à l'acceptation d'une monnaie unique pour une partie des membres de l'Union européenne.

Au plan économique, les économies nationales structurées par les pouvoirs publics se déstructurent face l'internationalisation du capital devenue la mondialisation. Les États doivent répondre à l'émergence de grandes structures internationales dont les objectifs et les champs d'action dépassent les cadres nationaux usuels : firmes transnationales, organisations internationales type OMC, ONG internationales.

Cette période est également celle de l'émergence et du développement des économies asiatiques le Japon puis les NPI (Corée du Sud, Taiwan, Singapour etc.). Elle sera suivie par le rôle économique international de la Chine suite aux réformes impulsées après l'échec e l'ultra-gauche.

Au plan politique et militaire, l'effacement du bloc socialiste puis de l'URSS fait disparaître une des raisons de la construction de la CEE tout en redonnant par ailleurs, au moins en France, une nouvelle actualité au risque de la reconstitution d'une puissance allemande autonome. L'affaiblissement de la Russie puis les processus en vue de l'adhésion d'États du CAEM ou de l'URSS marque la fin d'une alliance de fait entre les États européens et les États-Unis pour qui l'Europe occidentale perd de son importance stratégique.

Quelle place pour la CEE ? une zone de libre-échange au sein d'un monde devenu libre-échangiste n'a pas beaucoup de sens. Que peut signifier dans ce monde une construction régionale du type de la CEE ? Cette période nécessite de la CEE de repenser son fonctionnement et sa cohérence tout en devant trouver sa place au plan international. Cette période se traduit par un ensemble de réflexion permettant de penser la CEE au sein des relations internationales.

3 L'HEURE DES CHOIX

L'Acte Unique puis le traité de Maastricht modifie les conceptions de la construction européenne. La philosophie ancienne, comme nous l'avons vu, ne permettait pas de répondre aux défis du moment. L'alternative était simple, un maintien d'une régionalisation molle au sein du monde globalisé ou une construction volontariste d'une structure régionale pérenne. C'est la seconde branche de l'alternative qui a été retenue par la France en 1983, par l'Allemagne en 1989. Comment construire une entité européenne ? Dans un premier temps, il a semblé que le fédéralisme donnerait une réponse acceptable, c'est ce que signifiait le traité de Maastricht. Cependant, l'impossibilité de disposer d'une monnaie unique pour l'ensemble de l'UE, le grand élargissement avec l'affirmation des intérêts étatiques ont conduit à une autre voix pragmatique largement non théorisée.

4 UNE REDEFINITION DE LA CONSTRUCTION EUROPEENNE

Sur le plan économique, les traités successifs dépassent la logique du marché unifié pour intégrer des domaines plus larges de l'économie. La monnaie unique est emblématique de la volonté d'élargissement des domaines communautaire, la création de l'UEM, et de la BCE, semble affirmer une puissance voire un État européen. Il s'agit d'un processus inachevé tant que n'existe pas une régulation économique au plan de l'UE. La création d'une monnaie unique à vocation internationale en concurrence avec le dollar, la livre sterling et le yen induit une dimension d'Europe puissance à travers un rééquilibrage du système monétaire international. L'euro devrait occupe une place croissante dans les transactions internationales et comme instrument de réserve même si sa place reste inférieure à 20 % des réserves de change. La faiblesse de l'euro se situe dans sa représentation monétaire sur la scène internationale. La représentation dans les organisations internationales est plurielle, le président de la BCE pour les aspects monétaires, le président de l'euro 12 et les États membres pour les questions économiques, la Commission étant généralement absente. Au sein de l'Union européenne, la gestion de la monnaie a été voulue aussi peu politique que possible. E qui réduit d'autant la possibilité d'une visibilité internationale.

Les problèmes institutionnels ne permettent pas d'avoir une représentation unifiée sur le plan mondial. L'économie est largement du domaine de la Commission, la politique et le militaire ressortent du domaine du Conseil et suppose un accord à 25. La crise irakienne a démontré l'incapacité d'une position commune et d'une pratique commune.

Les choix de politique internationale restent du domaine des États. Au plan de l'affirmation des positions et des relations internationales, il existe une possibilité de conflit et d'opposition entre le commissaire et le représentant de la Pesc.

Le problème principal est celui des objectifs que se fixerait de l'Union européenne au plan international. Or les traités de Maastricht comme de Nice ne fixent pas de but précis sur le rôle de l'UE comme acteur global opposition-coopération avec les autres puissances mondiales (États-Unis, Russie, Chine etc.). Ils ne supposaient pas plus de position commune sur organisation du système international et le rôle de l'ONU.

Le Traité de Maastricht avec la distinction en trois piliers proposait une cohérence fictive qui n'a pas trouvé un mode de fonctionnement. Satisfaisant. La démarche de Maastricht se positionnait dans une tendance fédérale. L'euro est sans doute le plus clair symbole de cet engagement vers le fédéralisme. Il ne sera pas suivi, les appréhensions ou les espoirs exprimés sur la constitution d'un Etat fédéral européen se dissipent assez rapidement. Et ce d'autant plus vite que les élargissements envisagés ne permettent pas d'envisager l'acceptation par les Etats de l'Est européen de leur perte de souveraineté. L'incapacité des traités en vigueur de permettre la construction d'une entité européenne ont conduit à associer aux réflexions sur l'avenir de l'Europe les représentants des Parlements nationaux et européen aux États, acteurs habituels des CIG, le résultat en est le Traité de constitution une nouvelle forme de penser les interrelations entre les États membres.

5 L'AFFIRMATION DE L'UE

La démarche de Maastricht reste imprégnée de fédéralisme et de l'objectif lointain des États-Unis d'Europe. Les élargissements successifs, les traités d'Amsterdam de Nice et le traité de la constitution européenne signalent un recul de l'idée fédérale au profit d'une construction institutionnelle complexe. La recherche des convergences économiques elles-mêmes est abandonnée au profit d'une mise en cohérence des politiques des États membres, d'où l'importance de l'affirmation des principes généraux de la construction européenne. La convention une intégration plus de piliers donc pas de différences institutionnelles et politiques entre les champs des niveaux différents de communautarisation Les débats comme les discussions au cours de la Convention montrent clairement l'abandon de la construction d'un Etat fédéral. Le projet de traité de constitution explicite les différents niveaux de compétence entre les institutions européennes et les Etats membres sans que la perspective fédérale ne soit envisagée

Les relations internationales de l'Union Européenne se transforment en relations internes ou en relations de partenariat. Le processus d'expansion continu de l'UE tend à absorber les pays voisins soit directement au sein de l'Union européenne soit par l'adhésion à l'Espace économique européen dimensions économiques et politiques avec une organisation des relations économiques soit par des partenariats qui se transforment ensuite pour certains pays comme la Russie en accord spécifique. Le processus d'extension réduit en fait le champ des relations internationales. Ce modèle s'oppose au modèle plus classique de domination que l'on trouve aujourd'hui avec la politique des Etats-Unis. Le modèle européen s'analyse plus comme la structuration d'une économie monde que comme un Empire[1]. Les Etats gardent l'ensemble de leurs prérogatives, le Traité prévoit même pour la première fois une possibilité de sortie de l'Union. Le processus d'adhésion est d'autant plus facile que les Etats conservent leur identité. Les conditions d'adhésion, l'intégration de l'acquis communautaire, sont acceptables. Le non respect de l'acquis peut aboutir à un retard dans l'adhésion pas à un arrêt définitif. Contrairement à un Etat fédéral l'expansion de l'UE peut être envisagé comme un mouvement sans fin dans un processus d'expansionnisme démocratique[2]. La contrepartie de cette démarche est l'absence de centre clairement identifié et le recours à la négociation pour organiser les relations entre les Etats.

Des signes semblent indiquer que la préférence pour des concurrences intra-européennes se modifie vers une perception d'une concurrence mondiale. Nous n'en sommes certainement pas encore à l'heure de la constitution de champions européens, néanmoins la constitution d'EADS comme les autorisations de regroupements dans le domaine pharmaceutique, le refus du démantèlement de la PAC peuvent laisser penser à une inflexion des dogmes sur les niveaux de concurrence souhaitables.

6 CONCLUSION

L'échec du libéralisme à produire une régulation marchande au plan mondial comme à celui de l'Union nécessite d'élaborer les formes de régulation faisant intervenir les États et les puissances dont l'Union européenne. Au plan interne, l'Union doit construire les formes d'une régulation sous des formes à inventer dont les principes constituent les soubassements du Traité de constitution qui précise l'organisation des interdépendances en son sein. Au plan externe, l'Union européenne ne constituera pas un partenaire étatique, elle agira à travers les États la constituant avec des tensions et des discordances aussi bien que des concordances et des coopérations.

La construction européenne ne peut plus esquiver les choix sur son avenir. La fin de l'affrontement bipolaire, les avancées de la construction européenne, les contraintes de la mondialisation nécessitent une vision de long terme. Nous pouvons très

1 Braudel, Wallerstein

2 Pour reprendre les analyses que nous développons actuellement au sein du CUREI.

schématiquement résumer les différentes possibilités en deux options : le statu quo, une Europe puissance.

Le statu quo consiste à maintenir un espace économique sous forme d'un grand marché acceptant une structuration mondiale par les agents transnationaux et les EU. Une Europe dont les contours resteraient flous, dont l'identité serait multiple dans un espace complexe. Ce serait le cas dans l'éventualité d'un rejet du Traité de constitution. L'Europe se constituerait comme un modèle des droits de l'homme défenseur de valeurs universelles. Une telle attitude conduit à déliter l'Union européenne au sein de la mondialisation, dans une logique libérale.

La seconde possibilité est une Europe décidée à exercer des responsabilités internationales et à même de définir ses fonctions et de construire des relations diversifiées avec d'autres puissances dans son environnement proche ou lointain. Une Europe qui serait à même de définir son espace interne et de développer des relations externes. Elle suppose de définir où s'arrête l'Europe et où commencent les relations internationales. La définition des limites de l'Europe est un enjeu essentiel dans l'existence de l'UE comme acteur mondial. C'est aussi accepter des responsabilités dans les affaires internationales en tant qu'acteur. Est-ce envisageable ? Est-ce compatible avec le caractère toujours provisoire des frontières de l'Union qui caractérise la construction européenne ? Il s'agirait comme nous l'avons esquissé d'une puissance substituant la négociation à la force, sous réserve de disposer des capacités militaires lui permettant d'être crédible. L'Europe organiserait, sur son modèle, des interdépendances entre des États et des zones dans une vision en rupture avec la démarche classique de puissance. Une décision devient légitime quand elle exprime la volonté d'un peuple et qu'elle est acceptée par ses voisins L'Europe aurait vocation, non à s'affirmer en super puissance, mais en organisatrice au nom de principes universels des interdépendances entre elle-même et ses différents partenaires.

Bibliographie

Barrot (Jean), Elissade (Bernard), Roques (Georges) (2002, Europe, Europes, Espaces en recomposition, Paris : Vuibert, 3° édition.

Besson (Jean-Louis), Guillemin (Guy) (sous la direction), L'Europe puissance : entre virtualité et réalité, Les cahiers du Curei, n°16 janvier 2002.

Bitsch (Marie-Thérèse) (2001), Histoire de la construction européenne, Bruxelles : Complexe.

Cohen-Tanugi (Laurent), Le choix de l'Europe, Paris Fayard 1995

David (Dominique), « Vers quelle Europe ? Europe espace ou Europe puissance ? », Cahiers français, n° 298, p. 74 - 79

Dumond (Jean-Michel), Setton (Phillipe), La politique étrangère et de sécurité commune, Paris, La Documentation française, 1999, collection « Réflexe Europe »

Gerbet (P.), Barrot (Jean), La construction de l'Europe, Paris, Imprimerie nationale,1999

Gnesotto (Nicole), L'Europe et la puissance, Paris Presses de Sciences Po, 1998

Guisan (Catherine), Un sens à l'Europe. Gagner la paix (1950-2003), Paris : Odile Jacob, 2003.

Hobssbawn (E.J.), l'âge des extrêmes. Histoire du court XXe siècle, Bruxelles : Editions Complexes, 1999.

Larat (Fabrice) (2003), Histoire politique de l'intégration européenne, Paris : La documentation française, Les études de la documentation française.

Le Serre (Françoise de), Lequesne (Christian) (dir) Quelle Union pour quelle Europe ? L'après traité d'Amsterdam, Bruxelles, Éditions complexes, 1998

Leveau (Rémy), « Le partenariat euro-méditerranéen », Problèmes économiques, n° 2 686, 1er novembre 2000, p 1 - 6.

Lévy (J.), Europe, Une géographie, Paris : Hachette 1997.

Moreau-Defarges (Philippe), « L'Union européenne, la fédération-nébuleuse, Paris Note de l'IFRI, 1997

Pelletier (Pierre), « Intégration économique et accords de libre-échange », Problèmes économiques, n° 2 686, 1er novembre 2000, p 7-10.

Reboud (Louis) Économie européenne, Grenoble : PUG, 1996

Reboud L. (1996) Economie européenne. 1. Les limites de l'internationalisation des marchés. 2. Les conditions de l'intégration, Grenoble, PUG.

Silguy (Yves-Thibault de), L'économie fil d'Ariane de l'Europe, Paris : Presses de science Po, 2000.

Silguy (Yves-Thibault de)L'économie fil d'Ariane de l'Europe, Paris : Presses de Sciences Po, 2000

Tchakaloff (Marie-France Christophe), Les grandes étapes de l'organisation de l'Europe, Paris : PUF, QSJ ?, 1999, 2° édition.

Teyssier (François de), Baudier (Gilles), La construction de l'Europe. Culture Espace Puissance, Paris :PUF, 3° ed 2003, QSJ 3535.

Traité établissant une Constitution pour l'Europe, Paris : La Documentation française, 2004.

Tunander (Olan), « Post-cold War Europe : Synthesis of a Bipolar Friend-Foe Structure as a Hierarchic cosmos-Chaos Structure ? », in Geopolitics in Post-Wall Europe, Territory and Identity, editor by Ola Tunander, Pavel Baev, Victoria Ingrid image, Oslo : PRIO, 1997.

Zorgbibe Charles, Histoire de la construction européenne, Paris PUF 1993

DECISION-MAKING IN EU'S CFSP: DEFICITS AND PERSPECTIVES

REIMUND SEIDELMANN

1 THE PROBLEM

Within the catalogue of approaches to foreign policy analysis the actor-oriented approach constitutes one if not the classical approach.[1] The idea that actors translate structures and constellations, interests and norms, and power into specific actions/reactions allows not only a focussed empirical analysis but a better political focus in the understanding of the political process in general. Further, strategy- and tactic-building in politics are mostly actor-oriented; it is, for example, the actor, who decides with whom and in what way alliances and conflicts are pursued and solved.

In addition to such analytical advantages the actor-oriented approach has a major advantage over all structuralistic[2] and other approaches: it allows - or better demands - to integrate the decision-making process into the analysis, which leads to a major enlargement of its analytical scope. Decision-making means (1) the empirical analysis of structures, conditions, and dynamics of the decision-making process, (2) the processing of information and inputs either from the outside or the inside - and in particular the role of misperception -, and (3) the interrelation between the individual and the institutional factor. But further, the focus on decision-making within the broader actor-oriented approach allows to introduce two valuable analytical as well as central political concepts: the willingness and the ability to make decisions[3]. And although existing capabilities, range for activities, cost-benefit-risk relations, constellations, and normative settings already take into account will-building and ability-calculation, will and ability have to be regarded as prior, essential, and non-replaceable conditions for

1 For an overview of the most important theoretical approaches in foreign policy studies see for example Lehmkuhl, Ursula (Ed.): Theorien Internationaler Politik. Einführung und Texte. Munich: Oldenbourg, 1997, and also Krell, Gert: Theorien der Internationalen Beziehungen. In: Knapp, Manfred/Krell, Gert (Eds.): Einführung in die Internationale Politik. Munich: Oldenbourg, 2004, pp.57-90.

2 For a discussion of constuctivist and postmodern approaches in international and intercultural studies see Vasilache, Andreas: Interkulturelles Verstehen nach Gadamer und Foucault. Frankfurt am Main/New York: Campus, 2003.

3 This includes decisions to non-decide.

actors' action or non-action. Political will is not everything but without political will all other factors do not translate into action.

In addition, the actor-oriented approach is not only valuable for foreign policy but for international or intraregional relations analysis as well. Defining the international system as a system of different interrelated actors reaffirms not only the importance of actor-oriented analysis but demands to differentiate between different types, qualities, and profiles of those actors. If one looks at categories such as actors' will-building, ability, and economic, military, and political capacity to project the actors' political will into the international system, one can focus on the analysis of hierarchies of power within the international order to characterize the quality of the system as such. Again, this is not only important for scientific analysis but for policy-building and policy-realisation as well.

If one understands the EU's Maastricht Treaty as well as its post-Maastricht developments as a political process to transform the EEC/EC into a true global actor, if one defines Common Foreign and Security Policy (CFSP) as a framework including European Security and Defense Policy (ESDP) and related policies[4] and if one compares such an understanding of the EU as a true or relevant global actor with the realities of the past years there is a general understanding of a major gap between the proclaimed and the real role.[5] A differentiated view of the real impact of the EU on international relations can distinguish between the different dimensions and the different regions:

- There is no doubt that the EU is a major player in global economics - including monetary policies - both as an actor in itself as well as a member of institutions for global management such as WTO. But there is equally no doubt that the EU constitutes only a limited or marginal player when it comes to military power projection and in particular to global military power projection, and that the EU plays only a selective, occasional, and limited role in the setting of the global political agenda.
- And there is no doubt, that the EU is the dominant player in its "near-abroad"-neighbourhood, that it plays a significant and growing role towards major nation-states like the U.S., Russia, Eastern Europe,[6] and Japan and towards regions like

4 Such as establishing the EU Crisis Intervention Force and the preparation of a Common Armament Market.

5 See for example Peterson, John (Ed.): A common foreign policy for Europe? Competing visions of the CFSP. London: Routledge, 1998.

6 See Seidelmann, Reimund (Ed.): EU, NATO and the relationship between transformation and external behaviour in post-socialist Eastern Europe. The cases of the Slovak Republic, Bulgaria, Romania and Ukraine. Baden-Baden: Nomos, 2002.

Latin America,[7] Asia-Pacific, and Africa. But problems and conflicts like those in the Middle-East, the Gulf together with Afghanistan and Central Asia,[8] and with North Korea have underlined that the EU is by far not the global player it wanted or wants to be.

Thus, the EU as a global actor can be characterised by the dual-view-approach. Towards global affairs we can state the coexistence of will and ability and of non-will and inability of the EU at the same time. First, the EU is projecting power, interests, and norms towards its regional and international environment, thus replacing, complementing, or competing with traditional U.S. dominance. For example

- Peace-and-democracy-building in the Balkan and in Wider Europe as well as the very power-structure in the wider European region are clearly dominated, shaped, and controlled by the EU.
- The European Monetary Union (EMU) as one of the two major political projects of the Maastricht Treaties has quickly developed not only into a mayor player of the global monetary system but into an equal power partner to the U.S as well.

But second, the EU is unable to act as a global power, to project its interests successfully, and to succeed against or in partnership with the U.S. A rhetoric of challenging the U.S. contrasts with the EU's irrelevance in the management of international conflicts, the solution of global problems, and in the pursuit of better global governance. Examples are

- The non-existence of the EU/EMU with regard to solving financial-monetary crises such as the recent crisis in Argentine.
- The reactive pattern of the EU in the case of the fight against international terrorism, in the solution of the failed-states- or "criminal"-states problems, and in the question of widening and deepening non-proliferation.
- The no-role of the EU in cases of militarised conflicts or cases of malevolent states such as Iraq, India-Pakistan, North Korea, and Sudan.
- The political irrelevance of the EU within the United Nations System[9].

7 On this see Westphal, Kirsten, Biregionalism : Projecting a new pattern of governance? European Union's relations with Latin America; in: Seidelmann/ Grabendorff (eds.), The Relations between the European Union and Latin America: Biregionalism in a Changing Global System, Nomos:Baden-Baden, 2005, S.141-206.

8 See Giese, Ernst/Seidelmann, Reimund (Eds.).: Cooperation and Conflict Management in Central Asia. Frankfurt am Main: Peter Lang, 2004.

9 This has recently been documented in Germany's request for a German – and not a EU seat – in the U.N. Security Council.

The EU and more precisely the supporters of European integration explain this gap between the "two" EU's or between will and non-will by referring to the political principle of learning. They assume a theoretical doctrine of learning, i.e. to define the EU as a globalising power, which gradually complements its economic with military and political power and which develops from an inwards facing EEC towards a globally-oriented EU. But the advocates of the learning doctrine face the problem of how to establish a sustainable learning dynamic to replace learning-out-of-disaster- and stop-and-go-learning-curves. In addition, the look at the EU's resources, history, and new identity leads to the conclusion that such learning is less a problem of capacity-building but more of political will and ability of the EU's decision-making process. Again, the explanation of will-building is a major point in explaining why in the one case one faces an active EU and in the other case an unwilling and unable EU.

2 THE EU'S FOREIGN POLICY DECISION-MAKING DEFICITS

In the following this hypothesis - i.e. that there are major structural and historic as well as organisational and institutional deficits in the will-building and in the ability for common decisive policies - leads to two basic and interrelated explanations: the first one consists of the functional and historical nature of the EU as a supranational body and the second one is related to the institutional design and the organisation of the decision-making process for the EU's foreign and security policies.

2.1 The problem of decision-making as a supranational actor

Different to classical superstates like the U.S., the EU is not a super but a supranational actor. As a supranational actor in general and due to the specific history and nature of the EU in particular, the EU is first characterised by its cooperative as well as competitive duality between itself and its member states. And it is this general dual nature, which limits will-building and which produces a sort of "natural" lack in decision-making ability. Second, the EU's foreign and security policies show additional patterns and concepts, which further limit will-building and ability to decide.[10]

[10] On this topic see for example Jopp, Mathias (Ed.): Das Vertragswerk von Nizza und die Zukunft der Europäischen Union. Bonn: Europa-Union-Verl., 2001.

Nation-states in general and European nation-states in particular traditionally have a highly governmentalised foreign and security policy due to historical developments[11] as well as to functional necessities and public priorities[12]. Presidential systems as in France give foreign and security competences to the president and parliamentarian systems allow the prime minister or chancellor to marginalise the foreign and defense minister. All in all, foreign and security policies constitute "arcane" policies which are controlled by the governments and a relatively closed and government-oriented foreign and security "community". In addition, foreign and security policies carry a traditional sentiment of sovereignty-orientation. Although obsolete and anachronistic,[13] many European nation-states regard processes of acceptance- and legitimacy-building through symbolic actions or demonstrations of foreign and security sovereignty as important. And for some European states these policies were not marginal but used to define their national identity:

- Eastern European nation-states, which have suffered for decades from Soviet domination or lack of de-facto-sovereignty in foreign and security issues, used their new "independence" and sovereignty after the collapse of WTO and Soviet rule to reaffirm or to rebuild their new political identity.
- Neutral European nations regarded neutrality not only as a strategic concept, which made sense in specific historical situations such as the East-West conflict, but as an essential element of their peace-profile and their historic role for Europe.
- France as a mayor European player developed its Gaullistic concept of independence with its "force de frappe" as the ultimate symbol of independence.

11 One has to remember that the gradual transformation from the monarchic to the democratic state and the various compromises of power-sharing between monarchic and democratic forces defined in most cases foreign policy as the monarchy's last resort. In the final step of democratic transformation the now strong and experienced democratic government understood the advantages of limiting classical democratic control through parliaments, parties, and the public in foreign and security policies and established a sort of executive democracy in such policies. On this see Czempiel, Ernst-Otto: Kluge Macht. Außenpolitik für das 21. Jahrhundert. Munich: Beck, 1999.

12 Election analyses have made clear that voters give priority to domestic issues; taking foreign and security issues into account is a phenomenon, which is only case-oriented and of limited duration. For an empirical analysis of the attitudes of European citizens towards the CFSP see Kernic, Franz/Callaghan, Jean M./Manigart, Philippe: Public opinion on European security and defense. A Survey of European trends and public attitudes toward CFSP and ESDP. Frankfurt am Main: Peter Lang, 2002.

13 See Camilleri, J. A./Falk, J: The End of Sovereignty? The Politics of a Shrinking and Fragmenting World. Aldershot: Elgar, 1992.

The fact that the new independence of the Eastern European nations constituted no real independence but only left the option to join the West - i.e. EU and NATO - and that already during the East-West conflict formal neutrality of Scandinavian countries as well as Gaullism were based on a final de-facto-dependence on NATO's security guarantees indicates the ideological character of such policies. But it is a well-known phenomenon that ideologies and irrationalities - particularly in foreign and security policies - are more difficult to abandon, to replace, or to adjust than policies, strategies, and concepts, which are based on rational choice or rational cost-benefit-calculations.

Confronting such and other traditional sovereignty-sentiments in foreign and security policies with the political realities of European foreign and security policy leads to two observations, which further underline the gap between objective reality and subjective interpretations of that reality:

- First, security policy - including defense, military, and armament policies - of European nation-states was from the very beginning characterised by military integration or the transfer of national sovereignty: NATO membership meant to accept fullest military integration and far-reaching loss of national control. And while the end of the East-West conflict meant the end of the "Soviet threat" it did not mean the end of dependency on the willingness and capabilities of U.S. global military power projection.
- Second, while the foreign policies of European nations have never been integrated but continued to be based on bi- and multilateral coordination and harmonisation until the beginning of the CFSP project, they never could be regarded as independent or sovereign. Highly interrelated in an intra-European sense they were dependent on U.S. leadership - whether this led to anti- or pro-U.S. policies.

To sum up, European foreign and security policies after the end of the Second World War have never been really sovereign or independent. And policies pretending to be sovereign or independent in foreign and security affairs were not only unnecessary in terms of policy-formation but constituted ideologies which limited realistic evaluations of the scope and the geographical reach of these policies. In objective terms Maastricht's idea of integration referred to the existing realities, promised a much better cost-effectiveness, and aimed at a collective or common power and security-building, which would deliver the services the nation-state always promised but could never achieve. Turning back to the learning doctrine this means that the CFSP project reflects objective conditions, optimises cost-benefit-calculations, and maximises services. And if national foreign and security policies are therefore regarded as anachronistic, a functional analysis shows that their integration is not a question of interests and norms but of political will and ability to translate realities into politics. Nevertheless, the past and present EU integration process demonstrates that the EU's supranationality limits, delays, and sometimes prevents the development of political will to go for the necessary adaptation and that in the field of foreign and security policies this general lack of ability is particularly high.

The EU is not a functional but a historical entity as well. This means that in order to explain the specific state of CFSP and the integration of foreign and security policies in general, the functionalistic analysis must be complemented by a historical analysis based on the notion that political will is not only the result of necessities, interests, and norms but also of the historical factor as well. And the history of European integration shows that the dual character - i.e. integration and re-assuring the nation-state - explains the many contradictions and the stop-and-go-dynamic of the integration process. Supranationalism was never defined as a transition to supernationalism - i.e. a Europe similar to the U.S. - but as the necessary and sometimes unstable compromise between the objective necessity to integrate and the continued political will of the nation-state to exert as much influence as possible.[14] It has to be remembered that European integration has been and still is made less by supranational institutions such as the European Commission or the European Parliament but by the nation-states. They have the final say in any further integration steps and their parliaments ratify or reject all major advances in integration. The enlargements of the past and in particular the enlargement round of 2004 with ten new member states have further complicated common-will-building because of the growing number of decision-makers, their different engagement and professionalism vis-à-vis integration, and the growing heterogeneity of norms and interests reducing the common denominator, which is essential for the continuation of the integration process. This will be also the case for future enlargements.

Overall, there is not only a functional but a historical pattern in political will-building of European integration as well, which is characterised by the primacy of the nation-state's cost-benefit-calculation about advantages, costs, and risks of any further integration and the nation-state's strategy to keep as much competences, legitimacy, and resources in national hands as possible. Comparing the establishing of EMU with the implementation of the CFSP project illustrates both aspects. The EMU promised net-advantages as well as the repetition of the historical formula of integration to control Germany through integration. CFSP - and in particular the new situation after the end of the East-West conflict plus the transformation of NATO - did not promise such a net-advantage and furthermore seems not to be necessary in terms of the historical pattern. Therefore EMU was realised to its fullest extent while the CFSP project turned into the well-known stop-and-go, limited, and selective process.

14 That EU's continuous structural compromise between supranationalism and nation-state-orientation produces ambiguous and plurivalent policies and strategies is shown by Westphal, Kirsten, European Decision-Making towards Latin America: A Policy Approach of a Visionary Partnership or Anachronistic North-South Relations?, in: Seidelmann/ Grabendorff (eds.), The Relations between the European Union and Latin America: Biregionalism in a Changing Global System, Nomos:Baden-Baden, 2005, S.353-413.

In explaining will or non-will and ability and lack of ability, the nature as well as the history of the EU as a supranational actor - or the dual nature of the EU as composed of both supranational bodies and ideas and the national member-states and their understanding of national sovereignty - constitute the first and general limitation for will-building. Second, in the field of foreign and security policies historical sentiments as well as the comfort of a long-standing and in political, economical, and military terms cheap dependence on the U.S. and its global and regional services for Europe, for the EEC/EC, and for the EU constitute a further specific limitation for the will-building necessary to become a true global actor.

2.2 The institutional and political organisational problem of decision-making in the CFSP

In the case of the EU's CFSP and its related policies the dual nature of the and the above described 'cheap' dependence on the U.S. - both because of the very political nature as well as of the political history of the EU - limit common will-building and ability to decide when being translated into a specific political organisation and institutionalisation of the EU's foreign and security policies.[15] This means - in other words - that the EU's member states developed - and still show - a clear political will to continue the limitation of will-building and ability to decide, when it came or comes to foreign and security issues.

Again, the reference to the "duality" of the EU as a global actor illustrates and underlines the specific problems of the CFSP and related policies when the two major political projects of the Maastricht treaties - i.e. CFSP and EMU - are compared.

EMU as the successful model in terms of global actorship and in terms of will and ability rests on the following characteristics:

- the political approach of the "coalition of the willing", which automatically excluded the non-willing from decision-making;
- the choice of the integrated and not the intergovernmental model, which introduced majority voting and marginalised the power of member-states; and
- the one-dimensional and unambiguous institutional design with clear and full competences for the ECB and its President and its decoupling from the traditional decision-making process within and between the Council of Ministers, the European Commission, and the European Parliament.

15 See for example Regelsberger, Elfriede/Schoutheete de Tervarent, Philippe de/Wessels, Wolfgang (Eds.): Foreign Policy of the European Union. From EPC to CFSP and beyond. Boulder/London: Rienner, 1997.

CFSP and later ESDP plus the European Crisis Intervention Force followed a completely different design:

- they were based on a double-duplication approach: first, they did not substitute national foreign and security policies as well as military capacities but created an additional "supranational" policy and military force, and second, they did not substitute NATO or merged with European NATO but supplemented NATO's military capabilities with a small EU-European force;
- they did not follow the approach of the "coalition of the willing" but the approach of the traditional "all-member-states approach", which meant to depend not only on the consensus of the willing, less willing, and non-willing but also on the ability of the decision-making process to develop common positions above fundamentally different political-military profiles, traditions, and force structures;
- they were based not on an integrated but on an intergovernmental political design, which allowed member-states to dominate, shape, and in particular to delay, bloc, or sabotage common actions, and added not a fully integrated but a multinational force structure, which again allowed member-states to opt out from military missions or to prevent rapid build-up of this force through national financing patterns;
- they not only limited the power and competences of CFSP's High Representative but accepted an institutional competition between the European Commissions DG of External Relations etc. as in charge of economic instruments and the Council of Ministers as in charge of the political and military instruments of the EU's foreign relations; and
- finally they established a force structure, which is not only extremely limited in quantity but shows so many deficits[16] with regard to global military power or crisis-intervention projection, that it is not an "autonomous" European force but a minor and limited military capacity dependent for the foreseeable future from NATO and thus the U.S.

16 The most important are the lack of an effective C4, air transport capacity (probably until 2010), and global logistics.

The following scheme summarises this comparison between EMU and CFSP/ESDP:

	EMU	CFSP/ESDP
Political approach	"Coalition of the willing"	All member-states
Level of integration	Fully integrated	Intergovernmental
Institutional approach	One-dimensional (ECB)	Two-dimensional (Directorate General of External Relations with the Commissioner of External Affairs and the Council of Ministers with the High Representative for the CFSP)
Structure of the decision-making process	Hierarchical with the highest possible ability to act	Ambiguous, multi-layered, and consensus-oriented with a low ability to act
Effectiveness of decision-making and abilities	High/high	Low/low

Such multiple limitations for CFSP/ESDP and the EU Crisis Intervention Force in terms of will-building, ability to decide, and capacity to implement decisions must be confronted with three arguments:

- with EMU the political elite of Europe had a successful model and build-up strategy at hand, which could have easily been copied or applied to CFSP or - at least - to ESDP, and
- Europe's military and technological capacities as well as financial resources would have allowed to build a significant military capacity for global power projection, and
- NATO's military integration provided a highly successful model of merging national capacities into an effective military ability beyond national command and control.

To sum up, this means that this altogether again was a matter of explicit political will. In order to explain such lack of will one can refer to the above-mentioned nature and history of the European integration process as well as to the above-mentioned specific factors:

1) If one leaves aside the argument that the integration process after and because of Maastricht was already overloaded and that giving priority to EMU-building automatically meant to postpone or delay the implementation of the CFSP project, it seems reasonable to refer to the explanation that from the very beginning EU member-states - and eventually the European Commission as well - simply were not interested in a truly common or integrated CFSP together with an integrated

military capability and a Common European Armament Market because this meant an end to national foreign and security policies.

2) To explain the difference between the highly successful EMU and the not very successful CFSP project one can first refer to the basic mechanism of transferring sovereignty from European nation-states to the European Union in general and to the European Commission in particular. Both the rational-choice-approach - i.e. comparing the costs with the benefits of such a transfer and to support the transfer in the case of a clear net-advantage for the particular nation-state - and the historical approach - i.e. continuing a well-established and proven economic integration process with its early political formula to integrate Germany in order to control it - explain the support of the member-states for the EMU in general. But for the CFSP project these arguments were invalid. Joining and contributing to CFSP and ESDP meant high political and military costs and significant mission-risks particularly for the medium and smaller member-states. The problem of "German dominance" was non-existent because Germany's security policy and military capability were firmly under NATO control and showed decades of close cooperation and partnership.

3) In contrast to EMU, where the Europeanistic approach promised both the better pursuit of member-states' economic and monetary interests as well as the establishment of a true dipolar power structure, security policies were traditionally organised not in a Europeanistic but in an Atlanticist approach - i.e. NATO. In addition to this and despite all European criticism, NATO under U.S. leadership until now has provided and still promises to provide relatively cheap, politically comfortable, and low-risk security services - both within as well as outside the greater European region. Thus, traditional Atlanticism together with the "comfort"-factor, supplemented by U.S. foreign exchange pressures, resulted in a policy of choosing a "limited" CFSP/ESDP and European force capability.

Based on short-term political horizons, taking the costs and risks of CFSP and in particular of ESDP and the European force into account, referring to the problems of legitimising additional military expenditures and being reluctant to complement the EU's already far reaching economic power with alleged uncontrolled military power, the majority of member-states did not want to support a CFSP/ESDP model such as the EMU but opted for a model, a political organisation, and an institutional setting, which limited both the ability and the political will to decide on a common base and for a common policy to a minimum.

3 CHOICES AND PERSPECTIVES

Although these explanations for the basic deficits in the EU's foreign and security policy decision-making led to the conclusion that these are not created by chance but have resulted from the political will to limit will and ability of the EU's foreign and security policies, the principle of learning is still not proven wrong. Non-will or inability are not absolute but relative and depend on constellations, interpretations, and adaptation because of positive or negative learning experiences. In this regard, supporters of the learning doctrine cannot only refer to the EU's experience in the Balkan conflicts but rightly point to important changes in the decision-making process in the European Constitution that will, however, only enter into force if the European Constitution is accepted and implemented. Apart from the Constitution's major deficits in setting norms for the EU's foreign behaviour or global role etc. and despite its reconfirmation of the EU's duality, the creation of the EU Foreign Minister plus his or her empowerment because of the double position as the Foreign Minister responsible to the Council of Ministers and to the new President on the one hand, and as the Vice President of the European Commission on the other hand, has two major positive effects on will-building and ability:

1) it creates and legitimises a clear and unambiguous political responsibility in foreign and security affairs and significantly strengthens its position vis-à-vis the Council of Ministers; and
2) it overcomes the institutional competition between European Commission and Council of Ministers and establishes an institutional link between both, which significantly improves possibilities and chances of developing a "grand strategy" for the EU's global role, which effectively optimises its economic, military, and political instruments.

This means that these effects do not change the dual nature of the EU, the historical patterns of nation-states' behaviour, and the problem of double duplication but represent a major improvement in the efficiency of will-building and ability in the details of the decision-making process.

In addition to the Constitution, EU's new principle to allow coalitions of the willing within the Union in general and within the CFSP, the ESDP, and the EU Crisis Intervention Force in particular - and possibly in the case of a joint armament regime, too - is another major effect of the principle of learning. With such a new and generally legitimised method the EU re-establishes its ability to act despite the enlarged number of its member-states, increases its flexibility in political and military missions, and introduces the positive experiences made with the union-within-a-union model of the EMU into the CFSP/ESDP without basic changes. Additional references to the idea of establishing a European Security and Defense Union if the present system proves ineffective in the long run and to the idea of transforming NATO into a Two-Pillar-Alliance with the EU's CFSP/ESDP as the European pillar demonstrate that the EU's political elite is beginning to understand the problem in a more long-term and general mode.

Nevertheless, learning processes can but must not lead to improvement. Although the principle of learning is mostly regarded as a pro-integration dynamic, it can - and in particular with regard to the CFSP/ESDP and the EU force - lead to regressive effects as well. In this respect, from the perspective of the integrationists and supporters of the CFSP project three bad-case-scenarios can be taken into account, which might further limit the integration and intergovernmentalisation of the EU's foreign and security affairs:

1) The EU's crisis intervention mission can lead to large-scale political and military failure, which not only delegitimises the EU's crisis intervention policy in general but erodes its necessary domestic acceptance and support. Due to its sensitive nature and political weight CFSP, ESDP, and military crisis intervention in particular cannot survive without a minimum of public acceptance and elite support. Decline or erosion of the necessary minimum support would reduce CFSP/ESDP to political rhetoric.

2) Given the costly build-up of an autonomous military global power projection capability vis-à-vis the budgetary problems in the EU's member-states as well as in the EU itself and vis-à-vis simultaneous spending and resourcing for NATO and U.N. peace-keeping, financial support from member-states for the build-up and maintenance of its own military capability can be limited and downsized. Without a credible and effective force capability, however, CFSP/ESDP would again turn into a "paper-tiger", EU's global role would suffer, and dependence on U.S. global services revitalise.

3) NATO's "colonisation" of ESDP and the EU Crisis Intervention Force, together with coordinated U.S. efforts to re-establish NATO's prime role in intra- and extra-European security could undermine the effectiveness as well as the credibility of the CFSP/ESDP and the EU force. Again, this would not eliminate CFSP/ESDP and the intervention force but would - as in the case of Iraq - render it politically and militarily irrelevant.

The evaluation of such scenarios must again refer to the ability and political willingness of the EU in general - i.e. EU institutions plus member-states - to develop sustainable political will including the acceptance of decreasing short-term public support. But such political will has not only to deal with domestic conditions and dynamics. As in the case of the EMU, a politically able and militarily capable CFSP constitutes a direct challenge to U.S. global leadership. Even the doctrine of "Europe must become an equal and thus a better partner to the U.S." and the case of the EMU, where this doctrine has been successfully applied, cannot ignore that a EU with an effective CFSP/ESDP, with a credible global military power projection capability, and a comprehensive grand strategy, which successfully optimises political, economic, and military power means, leads not only to a relative decline of the global power of the U.S. but to an end to the

U.S. leadership monopoly in political and military global governance as well. Again, this is in the very end a question of political will - i.e. is the EU including its member-states willing and able to accept the costs, risks, and burdens of an active global role and is the EU willing and able to redefine its partnership with the U.S. in a constructive way and without a loss of Europe's new identity?

References

Camilleri, J. A./Falk, J: The End of Sovereignty? The Politics of a Shrinking and Fragmenting World. Aldershot: Elgar, 1992

Czempiel, Ernst-Otto: Kluge Macht. Außenpolitik für das 21. Jahrhundert. Munich: Beck, 1999

Giese, Ernst/Seidelmann, Reimund (Eds.): Cooperation and Conflict Management in Central Asia. Frankfurt am Main: Peter Lang, 2004

Jopp, Mathias (Ed.): Das Vertragswerk von Nizza und die Zukunft der Europäischen Union. Bonn: Europa-Union-Verlag, 2001

Kernic, Franz/Callaghan, Jean M./Manigart, Philippe: Public opinion on European security and defense. A Survey of European trends and public attitudes toward CFSP and ESDP. Frankfurt am Main: Peter Lang, 2002

Krell, Gert: Theorien der Internationalen Beziehungen. In: Knapp, Manfred/Krell, Gert (Eds.): Einführung in die Internationale Politik. Munich, Oldenbourg, 2004, 57-90.

Lehmkuhl, Ursula (Ed.): Theorien Internationaler Politik. Einführung und Texte. Munich: Oldenbourg, 1997

Peterson, John (Ed.): A common foreign policy for Europe? Competing visions of the CFSP. London: Routledge, 1998

Seidelmann, Reimund (Ed.): EU, NATO and the relationship between transformation and external behaviour in post-socialist Eastern Europe. The cases of the Slovak Republic, Bulgaria, Romania and Ukraine. Baden-Baden: Nomos, 2002

Seidelmann, Reimund/ Grabendorff, Wolf (eds.), The Relations between the European Union and Latin America: Biregionalism in a Changing Global System, Nomos: Baden-Baden, 2005

Vasilache, Andreas: Interkulturelles Verstehen nach Gadamer und Foucault. Frankfurt am Main/New York: Campus, 2003

Westphal, Kirsten, Biregionalism : Projecting a new pattern of governance? European Union's relations with Latin America; in: Seidelmann/ Grabendorff (eds.), The Relations between the European Union and Latin America: Biregionalism in a Changing Global System, Nomos: Baden-Baden, 2005, S.141-206

Westphal, Kirsten, European Decision-Making towards Latin America: A Policy Approach of a Visionary Partnership or Anachronistic North-South Relations?, in: Seidelmann/ Grabendorff (eds.), The Relations between the European Union and Latin America: Biregionalism in a Changing Global System, Nomos:Baden-Baden, 2005, S.353-413

RUSSIA IN MODERN INTERNATIONAL SYSTEMS: PROBLEMS OF MUTUAL PERCEPTIONS

ALEKSANDR N. NIKOLAEV

1 EFFECTS OF THE EU-ENLARGEMENT ON RUSSIA

It is rather remarkable that our conference is held in the days of a great historical event in the European development: the entry of ten European countries into the EU. This was undoubtedly an outstanding achievement, an important landmark on the way of European integration. However, it should be noted that this massive enlargement of the EU causes new large-scale political problems, both internal and external. It marks the beginning of the new stage in the EU-Russian relationship, also taking into account the recent enlargement of NATO.

The leaders of the united Europe and the leaders of Russia face the same challenge related to the strategy of further cooperation and the principles of its direction. Unfortunately we have to state that the policy of the EU towards Russia has no sharply focused strategic goals. Despite acknowledged importance of the Russian-EU partnership in different areas, the extent of Russian integration into the ever-enlarging EU has not been settled yet. On the other hand, the political elite of Russia is not unanimous about having "the Wider Europe" as a close neighbour and the emergent armed NATO forces at our borders. The European countries are the most welcome partners in the international arena. Russian foreign policy of 2003 has mainly focused on drawing nearer to the European Community. The Russian president V. Putin repeatedly underlined the priority of these steps. At the same time it has become obvious that the exaltation with regard to the "Russian-European choice" - its imminent entry into the highly developed civilization - has led to disappointment and doubts. The integration of Russia into the European Community proceeds slower than has been expected by the majority of Russians 10-15 years ago. The integration has exposed a number of certain obstacles in its way as well. The increasing gap between the uniting Europe and Russia in economic and political spheres stirs up a general concern of the Russian leaders. The present enlargement of the European Union brings about new economic, political, and humanitarian problems. Moscow top officials have never discouraged the entry of Central and Eastern European countries into the EU, but were reasonably concerned by a possible negative outcome as a result of the change of the EU's political geography.

The fears of Russia are connected with the unfavourable consequences of an EU enlargement. The former visa-free travelling of Russians throughout the majority of the Eastern European countries will be terminated. It is known that the aim of the signed agreement is not only to provide the freedom of travel across the EU, but also to increase control over external border-crossings by the citizens of non-member countries into the EU. This has brought about a stricter visa policy, applied to Russian citizens on all levels. A single strict standard includes more and more countries, which earlier used to pursue liberal visa policy. The trade of new member-countries from Eastern Europe will be retargeted and more oriented towards the home market of the Community. Russia has still no official warranty which validly acknowledges long-term contracts with these countries. A part of the foreign investments will flow into Eastern Europe instead of into Russia. The adoption of a single agrarian policy by the EU in these countries will inevitably prevent Russian agrarian exports and make Russian imports from these states expensive. The European enlargement will spread antitrust and antidumping EU legislature on the East European market. The member-countries will adopt the EU's technical standards and similar certification procedures. All this will become an obstacle for the Russian imports of mechanical engineering, chemical and food products. Apparently, the status of the Russian speaking population in the Baltic countries will not be equal when they enter the EU. Estonia and Latvia have not ratified the European social charter and frame convention on the protection of national minorities.

The issue of life sustainment in the Kaliningrad region seems to be the most distressful. First of all, it concerns transportation links with the rest of Russia, the visa regime for boarding cooperation, power supply and fishery. On the whole, the very idea of Russian integration into the European economic space in the nearest future seems rather unrealistic, as we do not meet a single one of Copenhagen's requirements or criteria. The alternative lies in a close cooperation between Russia and the EU. At present, Russia is somewhere outside of the integration process within the context of a "Wider Europe". The term "Wider Europe" itself reflects uncertainty with regard to the point of the Russian position in Europe. Solving this problem will help to avoid a new division of Europe and presupposes the introduction of new structures for gradual but consecutive Russian integration into new European institutions. This task seems even more vital with regard to the prospect of an EU and NATO enlargement involving the Baltic States, as well as the settlement of the Kaliningrad problem.

2 HISTORY OF RUSSIAN PREJUDICES

Along with the institutional divergences and differences in economic development levels, ideological and psychological factors play a crucial role in the Russian-EU relationship. All these factors, which are part of the mutual perception, are felt both in the course of contacts of common citizens and in the behaviour of the political elite, of businessmen, and the representatives of cultural work. Ideological and psychological prejudices in people's minds are mainly determined by historical reasons. The functional conformities of humane psychology have the specific characteristic that changes in the images of the object are not synchronized with the real changes in the object itself. Although other states are objects of high complexity, stereotypes seem to be one of the main forms of insight into the surrounding world in the minds of the masses. The most essential features of stereotypes are duration, conservatism, and determination by former knowledge about the subject, as well as a weak feedback with reality. The previous experience inevitably stipulates the perception of the object as a psychological basis of the stereotype. As a result, the mass consciousness of people interprets the relationship with any other country not only with regard to the present situation, but also in the light of the past.

And the past Russian-Western-European relationship has not escaped negative experience. Centuries-old historical experience of Russian people imposes the serious attitude towards defence issues. The idea "anything but war" in Russian policy was not formed by chance. Practically all wars, including victorious ones, came at a high cost. And if in our early history the most dangerous enemies came from the South eastern steppe, during the last three centuries evil and aggression came exclusively from the West. In the course of history we suffered German, Polish, Swedish, Italian, and English invasions. This could not happen without leaving a trace. Today we do not consider Western Europe as a firm image of the potential enemy, but subconscious suspicion remains. Religious contradictions are deeply rooted. For a thousand years Russia and Western Europe have professed different modifications of Christianity. Religion constitutes a basis for a civilized identity. The fact is that the Russian Orthodox believer considers the Western European citizen not only a foreigner but also as adhering to a different faith. Such insight is obviously a kind of misunderstanding. It does not only cover the natural psychological barrier between adherents of different confessions. In his famous work "Protestant ethic and the spirit of capitalism", M. Weber stated that each religion creates its own paradigm of activity in all spheres of inter-human relations. Orthodoxy and western branches of Christianity determined and shaped quite different images of the world and models of behaviour of the individual in it. We may argue the extent of difference between them, but one is unlikely to deny the fact that western Christianity is more oriented towards rationalism, individualism, and pragmatism. Prosperous businessmen have never been the role models in Russian culture. Saving of the soul has seemed more important than success in "earthly life". That is why we are more inclined to regard a thinker, worrier or sufferer as a positive hero. Several decades of Soviet atheism could not change these profound mental characteristics dramatically.

A similar attitude is observed in politics, art, and every-day life. The traces of it are substantial not only in the search for the ideal, but also in the conduct and evaluation of different situations. We differ in approaches to law and order, state, property etc. This leads to many misunderstandings both in professional and every-day contacts. The outstanding economist Keynes, a faithful friend of Russia, once wrote: "We cannot judge Russia on a sound basis ". Activity and attitude of the Russian Orthodox Church does not improve the situation. For a long time, Russia has been inaccessible for other countries, while even in the Middle Ages Western Europe had various and intensive contacts with different countries, started multinational families, established dynasties, its young people studying at the leading universities overseas. Today, mobility is a common thing for westerners. Throughout history, Russians considered foreigners as aliens from another world. A visit to a foreign country was a rare event. Changing the place of residence, even under exceptional circumstances, was regarded as treason. During the reign of Peter I the situation altered, primarily for the ruling elite, but that was only a small percentage of the whole population. Foreigners were still perceived as strange, alien, mysterious, and often hostile. This state of mind was made even worse under Stalin's regime and during the Soviet Era. Any trip abroad was authorized by a special commission of the Central Committee of the Communist Party in the late 1930s; a personal list of all delegates including technical staff had to be approved by the Political Bureau. In the 1960s-1970s the vast majority of Soviet people (excluding the citizens of Moscow and some big ports) had no contacts with foreigners. Only selected and reliable people had access to foreign specialists and had contact with tourists. One can hardly be surprised at the feeling of xenophobia in the modern Russian society after decades of such policy. Although xenophobia is not deliberately aimed at Europeans, it inevitably influences the relationship with them. Another result of total "isolation" was a poor command of foreign languages, as they were absolutely useless for the majority of people. At present, there is a psychological barrier concerning outside contacts for the senior and middle-aged generations. The consequences of the totalitarian ideological treatment of the Russian people during the Soviet Era should also be mentioned here. According to dogmas of communist propaganda, all western countries were referred to as the world of "rotten imperialism", which was the main source of evil on the planet. The struggle of socialism and communism was regarded as the pivot of all world events and capitalist countries seemed absolutely hostile. The famous American diplomat J. Kennen once wrote that the Soviet leadership described "the outward world as evil, hostile and threatening [...] which is doomed to perish due to increasing inner shocks [...] until the enhancing power of socialism delivers the last deadly strike." The image of countries which continued to make intensive war preparations, where a handful of tycoons exploited common people and where corruption and callousness reigned, was created deliberately. The whole system of ideological treatment - newspapers, journals, radio, TV and thousands of lecturers worked for it. Even animals of Durov's Circus revealed the ploys of world imperialism, e.g. a camel symbolized Charles de Gaulle. As a result of this propaganda strong negative attitudes and conceptions were moulded. Several generations experienced the impact of this policy. That is why many present Russian governors, representatives, scientists, and researchers in politics keep treating Western Europe based on the former and out-dated stereotypes.

3 MODERN EU-RUSSIA RELATIONS

Along with old prejudices, deeply rooted in history, against Western Europe there is one that emerged in the middle of the 1990s. It was a peculiar offence towards the West, the USA, and Europe and it emerged in direct correlation with the collapse of hopes that after the crash of the communist regime developed countries would "embrace" us, would welcome us in their community and help us to reach high living standards. This attitude was reflected in the statements of some politicians and outstanding public figures, emphasizing the fact that Germany owed us for our withdrawal of military troops. The attitude of the masses' minds changed rapidly. The 1991 poll of the Russian Information Centre of Public Opinion showed that 30% of all respondents called Western Europe a role model for development. In 1992 the result was 24%. Besides, the majority of Russian compatriots felt rather painfully the loss of the status of Super Power and considered the West to be to blame. The feeling of being a "besieged fortress" returned in the late 1990s. Everything mentioned may also be said of the Western European perception of Russia as something negative and oriented towards the past. This view is linked to the existence of the Soviet Union, for many years inspiring fear in the western world. This was proved by a recent survey and analysis of the contents of the western press by Russian researchers. It showed that first and foremost Russia is evaluated and gauged from the sight of its potential destructive impact on the world. Russia is regarded as a rather Asian power. The western mass media depict Russia as a cradle of terrorism, corruption, catastrophes, and potential conflicts. In general, the image of Russia is much more negative compared with that of Ukraine, Kazakhstan, and Caucasian countries. Everything positive reflects the past: cultural achievement, space exploration, military power. The situation may even become worse in the nearest future, due to the mass entrance of ex-Soviet republics into the EU. The post-Soviet syndrome in these countries is more tangible. All this may bring about certain obstacles to new initiatives on future cooperations with Russia. Questions of security may be especially damaging for us. They could dramatically influence a common favourable attitude of Russia to the European integration process and the NATO enlargement to the east. The differences in approaches and mutual perception are not an insuperable obstacle for integration. Moreover, countries of Western Europe enjoy the most positive image in the minds of the Russians. This is especially vivid in comparison with the image of the USA. We do not regard an anti-European attitude as something lasting, but anti-American feelings still exist among certain parts of the Russian population. Europe is regarded as the most desirable partner by Russia according to a survey of the All-Russian Centre of Public Opinion Studies. All these facts mentioned above are an integral part of the consequences of Cold War propaganda. The young generation, the students of our university in particular, regards Western European countries as rather attractive and friendly. Certainly, we have to get rid of the impact of the ideological factors of negative and outdated stereotypes. First of all, the proactive approach of the Russian elite with regard to the promotion of positive images of Russia on the mass media markets will encourage this process quite fundamentally. Secondly, the intensive mobility in educational and professional spheres will play an important role as well. The current level of partnership relations does not meet the needs of Russia and the EU. It demands a new quality in the field of strategic partnership. The number of geo-political factors - striving for entrance into the EU, the existence of an everlasting NATO expansion, weak integration links of post-Soviet states inside the CIS - should also be taken into account. In fact, two radically opposite variants can be offered. Further interaction will either reach the level of providing relative security on the continent or a strategic partnership will bring about a treaty of association with Russia. This option includes constant conflicts and the destruction of the CIS, expansion of Russo-phobia in Europe and of Euro-scepticism in Russia. In this case, prosperity and stability of Western Europe would hardly be achieved as long as the eastern part of Europe remained unstable and economically backward. Thus European integration should be aimed at bridging the gap between Europe and Russia. The second option is more preferable, although it collides with some political issues. The reshaping of the CIS is inevitable in the light of associated membership of Russia in Europe. The Asian countries of the Commonwealth will be excluded from the all-European integration process or viewed as minor EU partners. Russia will be forced to perform a bridging link between the EU and Asia. Even in the possible outcome one can hardly imagine Russia as a full member of the EU. The issues of Russia's European identity and the feasibility of its entrance into the EU should be clearly defined. Otherwise, we will face the danger of a collapse of all those integration structures and mechanisms that the "Small Europe" possesses today. A Russian membership in the EU will call for a fundamental reshaping of the latter. Cooperation on the level of associated membership seems most attractive. It will not involve a reshaping of the EU and the dissolution of the European states of the CIS, but will create the basis for the implementation of a Wider Europe project and will present the opportunity to integrate the Balkan countries into the EU, avoiding an intensification of contradictions with Russia. It will ensure enough time for the shaping of a new foreign policy strategy of Russia with regard to the relations with the Asian countries of the CIS. This agreement should consider the status of Russia, its role in ending the Cold War and its contribution to the antiterrorist coalition. The desired effect can be reached, provided the further transformation of the Russian economy and political system will follow the Western European model. Moving in this direction, Russia, “beautiful and careless child of the European family” (Keynes), will at last become its full and mature member.

References (translated)

Erofeev N.A. Foggy Albion. Britain and the English people in the eyes of Russians. Moscow. 1982

Keyns D. Brief glance at Russia/Socis, 1991 N7

Golubev A.V. "World Republic" on "Closed society": Soviet Union in 1920-30-s/ Russia and the World in the eyes of each other: from the history of mutual perception. Ed.2. Moscow, 2002

Kostomarov N.I. Russian customs. Moscow, 1995.

Stalin´s Politburo in the 1930s., Moscow, 1995

Kolosov V.A. Geopolitical picture of the world in mass media//Policy 2003., N3

Tikhomirov Yu. Security problems of Russia under Globalization//Power, 2004., N1

Aron R. Democracy and Totalitarianism. Moscow, 1993

Barghorn F. The Soviet Image of the United States. N.Y. 1950.

Brzezinski Z. Between two ages. N.Y. 1970.

RUSSIAN-EUROPEAN ECONOMIC RELATIONS: IMPACT OF THE ENLARGEMENT OF THE EU

OLGA GARANINA

1 INTRODUCTION

Cooperation between Russia and the European Union (EU) is of critical importance for the economic development of Russia. The EU is the largest economic partner of Russia. The accession of 10 countries to the EU in May 2004 (Poland, the Czech Republic, Hungary, Latvia, Lithuania, Estonia, Slovakia, Slovenia, Malta and Cyprus) modifies the economic and political map of Europe and forces a reconsideration of Russian-European relations. The enlargement of the EU reveals implicit contradictions inherent to Russian-European relations. Two main problems of Russian-European relations are: (1) the relative inequalities of Russian and European economic and political weight and (2) the incompatibility of deep economic integration with the preservation of political sovereignty in Russia and Europe. First, despite the weakness of its economic potential, Russia maintains political weight on the international scene. The EU, on the other hand, is often named an 'economic giant' and a 'political dwarf.' Second, the deepening of economic integration between Russia and the EU is compromised by the preservation of the political independence of the partners since Russia is not a candidate to the accession to the EU. Moreover, the enlargement of the EU entails numerous problems of a strategic order, such as the expansion of NATO, the participation of Russia in the European security system and the rights of Russian minorities in the Baltic States.

This paper presents an analysis of the economic aspects of Russian-European relations. Our objective is to study the current situation and the prospects for developing Russian-European relations in the context of the enlargement of the EU. The inequality of the economies of the EU and Russia explains the mismatches of the objectives and visions of mutual relations and the asymmetry of the trade and economic flows (2). The impact of the EU enlargement on the trade flows between Russia and the EU seems to be limited. In fact, the effects of trade diversion already took place in connection with the dissolution of the socialist states of Eastern Europe and of the USSR. Moreover, the average tariff in the EU is lower than in the acceding countries; and tariffs on imports of hydrocarbons and raw materials (which constitute the principal component of Russian exports) are usually low. Nevertheless, Russia refused to automatically extend the preferential agreements concluded with the EU to its new member countries (3).

If the effects of trade diversion seem rather insignificant, the enlargement of the EU will involve problems of a political-economic character related to the elaboration and enactment of external economic policy measures regarding zones of joint interest between Russia and the EU. It concerns, in particular, the new eastern neighbours of the EU (Ukraine, Belarus and Moldova) and the Kaliningrad region (4). As for the future of the Russian-European relations, the achievement of the Common European Economic Space project is complicated by the non-coherence of the deep economic integration with the adjustment of Russia to European norms and Russia's desire to conserve its political sovereignty (5).

2 RUSSIAN-EUROPEAN ECONOMIC RELATIONS: THE POLITICAL AND ECONOMIC INEQUALITY OF THE PARTNERS

Russia and the EU have different economic weights (2.1). The inequality of Russian and European economies explains the non-coherence of the legal framework of their mutual relations (2.2) and the asymmetry of their trade and capital flows (2.3).

2.1 Inequality of the economies

Russian-European relations are characterized by a high degree of economic asymmetry. Russian GDP constitutes approximately 4% of the GDP of the EU-15 on the exchange rate in current prices and 11% on purchasing power parity in 2002[1]. Real GDP per capita in Russia constitutes approximately one-third of the European level. After the enlargement of the EU, difference in living standards will remain; real GDP per capita in Russia will constitute less than 40% of the average level in the EU (Samson, Greffe [2002]).

The devaluation of the Russian ruble in August 1998 promoted a revival of Russian manufacturing. However, raw materials and energy still represent two-thirds of Russian exports. Russia has comparative advantages[2] in hydrocarbons, some products of natural resources (*e.g.* wood, pulp and paper) and energy intensive products (*e.g.* non ferrous metals, steel, fertilizers). The comparative advantages and disadvantages of Russian economy are deepening, and the list of sectors in which Russia is advantaged is quite short (Ahrend [2004]). Russian economic growth has been primarily based on

1 IMF: International Monetary Fund, World Economic Outlook Database, September 2004, http://www.imf.org.

2 Revealed comparative advantage: ACRi = (Xi/ΣXk –M/ΣMk) *100, Xi et Mi are respectively exports and imports of the product i.

the dynamics of its export branches. Russia seems to be unable to overcome its historical pattern of natural resource-based economic development.

The recognition of Russia as a market economy (September 2002) is one of the major successes of Russian-European economic cooperation. Thanks to this status, Russian companies can protect their interests on the basis of their real costs, instead of protecting them on the basis of the expenses estimated according to parameters of third countries. However, the EU continues to apply antidumping tariffs with regard to some of Russia's exports, including metals and chemical products. The asymmetry of the economies leads to a well-defined, but mismatched legal framework of economic relations.

2.2 Legal basis of the partnership: the incoherence of principal documents

Russian-European relations are based on the Partnership and Cooperation Agreement of 1994 (PCA, entered into force on 1 December 1997) aimed at encouraging political, commercial, economic and cultural cooperation between Russia and the EU. One of the purposes of the PCA is to promote the creation of a free trade zone between the EU and Russia. Both sides accord each other a most-favoured nation treatment (art. 10). Among the other purposes of the PCA are the support of democracy and a market economy in Russia, as well as the development of political dialogue.

The PCA provides the institutional framework for Russian-European relations. Specifically, it consists of: top-level summits between the EU and Russia twice a year, the annual Cooperation Council on the ministerial level[3], the Committee for parliamentary cooperation, and the dialogue among senior Russian and EU officials. The presence and functioning of the given institutions constitute real political effects of the PCA. According to A. Lynch ([2003], p. 58), however, institutional links are too bureaucratic and are more likely established by the needs of the EU, rather than by the nature of relations (for example, the frequency of summits is defined by the rotation of the presidency in the EU). Thus, as P. Sutela ([2003], p. 54) believes, the frequency of summits leads to virtual initiatives and an absence of real progress in developing relations. Moscow relates the difficulties of economic cooperation to a shortage of coherence in the dialogue. In fact, Vladimir Putin has declared that "it is difficult to work" with the EU because "every half-year its chairman and priorities change"[4]. Thus,

3 At the St Petersburg Summit of May 2003 it was decided to transform the Cooperation Council into a Permanent Partnership Council.

4 Citation from Suslov, D. "V Evrope ne poniali nedovolstva Kremlia", Nezavisimaya Gazeta, 30.03.2004, www.ng.ru.

the development of bilateral relations between Russia and individual EU member-countries is a way of circumventing the lack of continuity in Russia's relations with the EU's central bureaucracy. Finally, the slow advance of economic reforms in Russia also complicates the progress of the PCA. The initial duration of the PCA is 10 years (it is re-conducted automatically unless either side gives notice to the contrary), so its eventual re-negotiation will reflect the relations of an enlarged EU to Russia and will allow consideration of the future of the Russian-European relations.

Russia is included in the EU's circle of friends. The strategy of the EU concerning these countries is based on the principle of "cooperation without participation in institutions". The strategy of the EU can be characterized as a balancing act between including Russia in Europe because of its economic potential and excluding it, as Russia is not a candidate for accession to the EU (Bayou [2002], p.7). In 1999, soon after the crisis of 1998, the EU adopted the Common Strategy on Russia. The strategic goals of this EU strategy regarding Russia are the following: (1) the stability of Russia's democracy, rule of law and market economy, and (2) the stability and security of Europe and of the world. Thus, the transformation of Russia is declared among the main objectives of the EU, and the EU insists that Russia should adopt European norms. However, the EU's demands seem unfounded since Russia has not applied for accession to the EU. These institutional changes are not a necessary condition for the export of Russian products to the EU (Lynch [2003], Hamilton [2003]).

Concerning Russia's own outlook on relations with the EU, the strategy of the development of the Russian Federation's relations with the European Union for the medium term (2000-2010) is aimed at the construction of a Europe without lines of division, at the protection of Russian national interests, and the elevation of Russia's role in Europe and in the world. The first stage of this integration is the creation of a free trade zone between Russia and the EU. This strategy reflects Russia's anxiety over the enlargement of the EU. The negotiations on the enlargement were supposed to protect the interests of Russia. But if the EU's strategy seeks to have European standards take root in Russia, the Russian strategy will be aimed at the protection of its national interests. The disproportion of the Russian-European relations can be observed not only through analysing the legal framework of cooperation, but also through the analysis of economic relations.

2.3 Asymmetry of economic relations

The EU is the largest trading partner and the first source of foreign investments and foreign aid for Russia. In 2002, the EU accounted for 35.3% of exports from and 36.9% of imports into Russia. The dependence of the EU on the Russian market is less obvious: in 2002 Russia provided 4.8% of the EU's imports and was the recipient of only 3.05% of the latter's exports. Overall, Russia ranked as the fifth largest trading partner of the EU[5]. After the enlargement, the EU's share of Russia's foreign trade activity surpasses 50%. In fact, the ten new member countries play an important role in the structure of the international trade relations of Russia. In 2003, the new member countries delivered 7% of Russia's imports and bought 12% of its exports. Russia, in turn, provides only 3-11% of the imports (except for Lithuania to which Russia provides 22% of imports) and 1-5% of the market for these countries' exports (except for Lithuania and Estonia which send to Russia 10% and 11% of its exports respectively)[6]. However, the dynamics of trade relations depend mainly on a rise in prices for hydrocarbons.

The energy sector is of strategic importance for the Russian-European relations. The share of energy products constitutes 55.5% of the Russian export to the EU-15. Europe is the largest market for Russian energy resources. 45% of Russian energy exports (precisely, 53% of oil exported and 36% of gas exported) go to the EU. In turn, Russia provides 41% of the natural gas imported by the EU (19% of the total EU gas consumption) and 21% of net oil imports of the EU (16% of the EU total oil consumption)[7]. The energy dialogue which affirmed the importance of energy products in the economic relations of the EU and Russia was proclaimed in October 2000. European exports, on the other hand, are more diversified and consist mainly of manufactured goods (see Table 1).

Table 1: Structure of Russian-European trade relations

Russian exports	European exports
55.5% - energy and fuels 4.8% - agricultural products 4.0% - chemical products 3.0% - iron and steel 0.6% - textiles and clothing	16.5% - power generating machinery 13.1% - chemical products 12.1% - office machinery and telec. equipment 11.6% - agricultural products 10.1% - transport material 5.6% - textiles and clothing 1.3% - iron and steel

Source: European Commission, Market Access Sectoral and Trade Barriers Database. http://mkaccdb.eu.int. Consultation: 03/17/2004

5 See European Commission, www.europa.eu.int .

6 UN Comtrade Database, no data for Malta in 2003. Consultation : May 2005.

7 Data from: "Energy security : The Role of Russian Gas Companies", International Energy Agency –Soyuzgas Conference, November 25, 2003.

As for the structure of Russia's trade flows with the ten acceding countries, the domination of energy products is even more obvious than in the trade with the EU. In 2003, energy constitutes 30% of imports of Estonia, 43% of imports of Latvia, 57% of Slovenia and 66-88% of the imports of the other new member countries from Russia. Russia provides 40-97% of energy imports of the new member countries, except for Slovenia and Cyprus[8]. The export goods of the acceding countries are primarily manufactured goods which constitute 50-80% of all exports (see also Hamilton [2003]). Thus, the stability and growth of Russian exports to the EU depend on the dynamics of the Russian exports of energy products and on the diversification of the Russian economy.

So, the inequality of the relative political and economic weights of Russia and the EU is the cause of discrepancies in the mutual perception of the partners and in the comprehension of objectives of the cooperation. This mismatch is reflected in the basic documents defining legal and strategic frameworks of the relations. C. Hamilton ([2003], p. 24) believes that the EU's interest in developing economic cooperation with Russia is, except for natural gas, mainly founded on geopolitical considerations. Russian interests are more grounded on the economic sphere.

3 ECONOMIC IMPACT OF THE ENLARGEMENT IS LIMITED

According to the European Commission, the enlargement of the EU offers a new possibility for the development of the Russian-European economic cooperation and for the modernization of the Russian economy (2.1.). Russia, in turn, is afraid of the potential trade diversion effects. These trade diversion effects, however, seem to be improbable. Nevertheless, Moscow demands compensation for trade losses caused by the enlargement of the EU as condition for the extension of the PCA on the new member countries (2.2).

3.1 Impact of the enlargement: official point of view

The ten new members apply bilateral agreements of the EU, the common external tariff and the defensive trade measures of the EU, and refuse the bilateral agreements concluded with third countries.

8 ITC 3 Rev.3, data of 2003, UN Comtrade Database, no data for Malta. Consultation : May 2005.

First of all, the enlargement implies deep transformation processes for the EU. Thus, the complexity of the Russian-European relations will increase. Among the effects concerning Russia directly, it is possible to select the following effects (see for ex. Liikanen E. [2003]):

1) the share of the enlarged EU in Russia's foreign trade surpasses 50%. Thus, Russian companies entering into the European market will have access to a common market with 25 million firms and 450 million consumers. Both production and consumption standards will be harmonized and Russian companies will obtain the possibility to work on a uniform legal playing-field;
2) the accession to the EU entails changes of tariff barriers of the new member countries according to the European standards. The economy of the EU-15 is more open. The average tariff in the EU-15 constitutes 4%, while in the acceding countries it is about 9%. Among the acceding countries, only Hungary accorded Russia a most favoured nation treatment. Thus, Russian exporters will obtain important benefits due to the enlargement of the EU;
3) and finally, the expected economic growth in the EU after its expansion will promote the Russian-European cooperation in the field of trade and investments, particularly in the frontier regions.

Hence, the enlargement of the EU can have a positive effect on the growth and modernization of the Russian economy. According to studies of the institutes CEPS and RECEP, however, the enlargement will result in a growth of welfare of only less than 2% in Russia. Moreover, Russia expresses fears of trade diversion effects.

3.2 Trade diversion?

Trade diversion effects, and hence the losses of Russian exporters, seem to be improbable. First, the diversion of trade flows has already taken place in the wake of dissolution of the COMECON. The countries of Eastern Europe profit from a privileged access to the European markets within the framework of the European agreements concluded in 1991-96 and have reoriented their trade flows in favour of the EU.

Second, the stability of the volume of Russian exports is assured, because it is mainly composed of raw materials and energy products. Import tariffs on these products are usually quite low (Hamilton [2003], p. 10-12). Moreover, the harmful effects of trade diversion on Russia are less probable because the average level of tariffs in the new member countries will decline. Concerning the influence of the EU's enlargement on inward investment flows, the effect of investment diversion seems to be improbable. Foreign direct investment in Russia is principally directed at the natural resource extraction sectors or at the primary processing of natural resources. It can also be justified by the proximity to the final consumer. Hence, Russia and the new member countries do not seem to be direct competitors in attracting this type of inward investment. As for the Russian investments in the EU, their volume remains rather limited.

The enlargement of the EU entails a question of the extension of the PCA to its new member countries. The EU has demanded of Russia the extension of the PCA to the new members without any conditions or differences. Russia, in turn, has aspired to compensate for the trade losses caused by the enlargement of the EU (150 - 300 million dollars a year according to Russian estimations). The negative economic impact of the enlargement for Russia can be explained as follows:

1) First, tariffs applied by the new members to some products of Russian exports will be increased. A significant part of Russian exports to the countries of Eastern Europe was originally assessed with a zero tariff or the tariffs were lower than in the EU (for example, aluminium in Hungary and Lithuania was assessed with the zero tariff whereas in the EU the tariff is 6%).

2) We can expect a more active application of antidumping measures with regard to Russia. All antidumping barriers of the EU will be extended to the new members.

   An increase of quotas on some goods of the Russian exports (e.g. steel, grain) should be negotiated in connection with the enlargement.

   The policy of diversification of import sources of energy can have a negative effect on the Russian export of hydrocarbons.

   The transit of goods and people through the territory of the Baltic countries will become an important issue of consideration.

3) And finally, additional compliance expenses will arise for Russian companies, as the acceding countries will harmonize their standards with the technical, sanitary and phytosanitary, and economic standards of the EU.

In April 2004, Russia and the EU achieved a compromise on several basic issues including the increase of steel quotas, non-application of limitations on the deliveries of hydrocarbons from Russia, compromise level of tariffs on aluminium. The negotiations regarding the enlargement of the EU were conducted parallel to the negotiations regarding the accession of Russia to the WTO (the market access deal was signed on 21 May 2004). Thus the consent of the EU concerning the conditions of the accession of Russia to the WTO, notably the framework of development of the Russian energy sector, serves as a lever of pressure upon Russian diplomacy. Another issue of negotiations, the Kyoto Protocol, was ratified by Russia in October 2004. Tension in Russian-European relations is connected to the strategic changes concerning the governance of zones of joint interest in Europe.

4 IMPACT ON POLITICAL-ECONOMIC DIALOGUE

The enlargement of the EU contributes to the development of misunderstandings in Russian-European relations. The EU appears to be disappointed by the results of economic reforms in Russia and inculpates the latter of non-compliance with the principles of democracy and human rights. The cooling-off of relations between EU-25 and Russia can also be connected with the persisting negative perception of Russia in Eastern Europe. Among the political-economic problems directly connected with the process of the enlargement of the EU, the most important, in our opinion, are the coordination of Russian and European policies with respect to the new neighbours of the EU (3.1.) and the development of the Kaliningrad region which is becoming a Russian enclave in the EU after the enlargement (3.2).

4.1 Policy of the EU with respect to its new neighbours: Ukraine, Belarus, Moldova

The enlargement of the EU generates the question concerning the elaboration and realization of a policy with respect to its new eastern neighbours Moldova, Ukraine and Belarus. The incomplete character of economic reforms of the transition period and the variety of developing economic and political systems makes policy in this region very complex. Moreover, despite its economic weakness, Russia has kept its political role in Europe. Hence, the main problem remains to be the coordination of the Russian and European policies concerning those countries which can be counted as traditionally belonging to the sphere of Russian interests.

The presidential campaign in Ukraine revealed the crucial importance of this issue. Actually, Ukraine is politically shifting towards the EU, but economically it is still largely dependent on Russia which provides about 61%[9] of its energy imports and controls up to 55 % of foreign investments in Ukraine[10]. So, Ukraine is actually seeking to diversify its energy imports, in particular with the recourse to the reserves of the Caspian Sea.

It should be noted that both Russia and the EU are interested in the development of this region, and primarily in maintaining stability in the region and in the functioning of its infrastructure - oil and gas pipelines, in particular (Haukkala [2002], Bordachev [2003]). Since 2002, the goal of the EU has been to develop a new initiative of good neighbourhood (or a "Wider European Neighbourhood"). Within the framework of this

9 SITC 3 Rev 3, UN Comtrade database, consultation : March 2005.

10 "Yuschenko's problems", Johnson's Russia list 9073 (source: Moskovskii komsomolets, No 55, 16 mars 2005).

initiative the new strategy and instruments of the inter-boundary cooperation are elaborated in more detail.

The Kaliningrad region represents a specific case of inter-oscillation and overlapping of the spheres of interests of the two European powers.

4.2 Kaliningrad: the enclave of Russia within the territory of the EU

The enlargement of the EU reveals the problem of the Kaliningrad region which becomes an enclave of Russia in the territory of an enlarged EU. The unique geographical position of the region and the status of this special economic zone entails a high degree of the region's economic openness and its specialization in the import of consumer goods and the further resale of imported goods to Russia.

The enlargement of the EU impedes the frontier trade and transit of goods to Russia which actually provide for the development of the region. At present, agreements on simplified customs rules have been adopted. So, according to the agreement achieved on the transit of goods, Russia is exonerated of customs duties on the territory of Lithuania. An agreement on the simplified mode of transit of Russian citizens has also been achieved. Nevertheless, the enlargement of the EU necessitates the conception and the realization of a strategy for the development of the enclave aimed to overcome the economic backwardness of the region.

The continuous process of the European integration poses a question with regard to the prospects of the Pan-European integration or, more precisely, one with regard to the perspectives of the Common European Economic Space.

5 PERSPECTIVES OF RUSSIAN-EUROPEAN RELATIONS: COMMON EUROPEAN ECONOMIC SPACE

The Russian-European integration evolves towards a creation of four Common Spaces: (1) A Common Economic Space, (2) A Common Space of Freedom, Security and Justice, (3) A Common Space of External Security, and (4) A Common Space of Research and Education, including Cultural Aspects. The negotiations on the Common European Economic Space (CEES) were launched in May 2001. CEES' objectives are to provide four fundamental freedoms (freedom of the movement of goods, services, people and capital), and also the development of competition and cooperation in numerous areas, such as research activity, protection of the environment, education and social policy.

In the opinion of European experts, the creation of the CEES should favour the coordinated development of their complementary economies. The CEES should be considered as a trajectory of a co-development path (Samson, Greffe [2002]). It would provide the diversification and modernization of the Russian economy, and the expansion of resource potential and commodity markets for the EU.

A package of road maps setting the goals of relations in the framework of the four Common Spaces and the actions for the middle-term perspective was adopted during the 15th Russia-EU Summit on 10 May 2005. So, in the economic area, the road map provides an objective of an open and integrated market thanks to a regulatory dialogue on industrial products, cooperation on investment issues, competition and financial services, and also cooperation in the field of telecommunications, transports, energy, environment and outer space activities. However, these provisions rather represent preferences of the partners than a definite plan of actions, and do not introduce crucial changes in comparison with the PCA[11].

The concrete form of this regional block has not yet been defined. It could become a free trade zone or it could be structured with an even deeper degree of integration. The special interest of the concept of the CEES consists of the combination of a deep economic integration with the political sovereignty of its members. The problem of balance between economic integration and political independence is one of the key problems in international political economy. So, in order to explain this problem, D. Rodrik builds a political trilemma of world economy[12]. At the top of the trilemma are the following: (1) integrated national economies, (2) nation-states (independent territorial and legal units) and (3) mass politics (political systems founded on unrestricted suffrage, a high degree of political mobilization and representative political institutions). It is possible to simultaneously realize two of these three aspirations, but not all three at the same time. Therefore, it appears impossible to guarantee economic integration and the state of law in Russia while conserving political independence.

Russia is not a candidate for accession to the EU; therefore it is extremely difficult to construct a system of institutions which would provide the constant adaptation of the Russian norms according to the European principles. For this reason, the creation of a free trade zone according to the PCA of 1994 should become the priority. This objective seems to be more precise and realistic. Furthermore, achieving it will allow the removal of the existing trade barriers on, for example, steel, as well as on agricultural, textile and chemical products.

11 Bykov P., Vlasova O., Kokcharov A. [2005] : "Pochemu my ne spechim v Evropu", Expert, 18, 16 May. www.expert.ru.

12 Rodrik D. [2000]: "Governance of Economic Globalization" in. Nye J.S, Donahue J.D. (eds.) [2000]: "Governance in a Globalizing World", pp. 347-365.

6 CONCLUSION

Russian-European relations are characterized by a high degree of economic and political asymmetry. If Russia aspires to provide the funds necessary for the macroeconomic stabilization and modernization of the economy, the EU will above all be interested in ensuring stability of the deliveries of hydrocarbons. The impact of the enlargement of the EU on trade flows seems to be rather limited. In fact, the trade diversion effect has already taken place in connection with the dissolution of COMECON and of the USSR. Tariffs in the EU are lower than in the acceding countries and are usually insignificant with regard to energy resources and raw materials. Nevertheless, the Russian exporters will face the problems connected with the harmonization of norms and standards and also with the application of the antidumping measures by the new EU member countries. The enlargement of the EU includes problems of governance of the zones of common interest. In many respects, the development of Russian-European relations depends on how the economic integration and political independence of the different sides will be counterbalanced.

The combination of the Russian economy's weakness and of the conservation of political power and political ambitions are subject to the contradictions of the Russian-European relationship. The tension in Russian-European relations is not only caused by the process of the enlargement's direct influence on Russian economy, but also by the weakness of the economy and state of law in Russia. Therefore, the problem of the consolidation of internal sources of economic growth and internal reforms are Russia's current priorities. The realization of this task will define a future role of Russia in the global economy and the development of Russian-European economic relations.

References

Ahrend R. [2004b]: "Russian Industrial Restructuring: Trends in Productivity, Competitiveness and Comparative Advantage", OECD Economics Department Working Paper, September. www.oecd.org/eco.

Bayou C. [2002] : "Les relations Russie-Union Européenne. Vers quelle intégration ?" Le courrier des pays de l'Est, 2002, mai, n°1025, pp. 4-16.

Bordachev T. [2003] : "Strategy and strategies", in Moshes A. (ed) [2003] : "Rethinking the Respective Strategies of Russia and the European Union", Special Finnish Institute of International Affairs - Carnegie Moscow Center Report 2003, pp. 31-61.

Hamilton C.B. [2003] : "Russia's European Integration: Escapism and Current Realities", Centre for Economic Policy Research (CEPR) Discussion Paper No 3840, March 2003. www.cepr.org/pubs/dps/DP38040.asp.

Haukkala H. [2002] : "Towards a Union of Dimensions. The effects of eastern enlargement on the Northern Dimension", Finnish Institute of International Affairs Report 2/2002. www.upi-fiia.fi.

Liikanen E. [2003] : "The Enlargement of the EU: Impact on the EU-Russia bilateral cooperation", 5th EU-Russia Industrialists' Round Table, Moscow, 1 December 2003. www.europa.eu.int

Lynch A. [2003] : "La Russie face à l'Europe", Cahiers de Chaillot, Institut d'Etudes de Sécurité, Union Européenne, Paris, n°60, mai 2003. www.iss-eu.org.

Samson I., Greffe X. [2002]: The White Book "Common Economic Space: Prospects of Russia-EU Relations", Russian - European Centre for Economic Policy, Moscow, October 2002.

Sutela P. [2003]: "Russia and Europe: Some Economic Aspects", Carnegie Moscow Center, http://www.carnegie.ru/ru/pubs/books.

KEY PROBLEMS IN RUSSIA'S NEGOTIATIONS FOR ACCESSION TO THE WTO

DAVID A. DYKER

Abstract

Russia has been negotiating for accession to the WTO for twelve years, and there is still no prospect of an immediate conclusion to the process. The reasons for this are partly to be found in the international environment. In the 1990s, the geo-strategic concerns of the Western powers created barriers to Russian integration into global trading structures. Even in the post-September 11 environment, existing WTO members have continued to use the WTO accession process as a way of advancing their own commercial policies vis-à-vis Russia. But the main obstacles to speedy accession have been internal. While the Russian government as a whole is strongly in favour of WTO accession as a way of strengthening the market mechanism and reform processes within the country, significant elements within it are equally strongly in favour of high levels of protection for specific sectors, on national security and/or technological/infant industry grounds. While the Russian business community as a whole is divided over the merits of accession, the powerful manufacturing and banking lobbies are demanding levels of protection that would be incompatible with accession. Russian views of WTO accession vary widely, within both government and the business community, and anyone who would lobby in favour of accession within Russia must bear this firmly in mind.

1 INTRODUCTION

The Russian Federation has been negotiating for accession to the World Trade Organisation (initially to the pre-Uruguay Round GATT) since 1993. It submitted its application in June of that year, and the Working Party on the accession of the Russian Federation was set up on 16 June 1993. The government of newly independent Russia was, in fact, simply picking up where the last Soviet government, had left off. The process of negotiation over the succeeding twelve years has been an intermittent one. Notably in the late Yeltsin era, Russia seemed to lose interest in the whole business. With the advent of the Putin presidency in early 2000, the commitment of the Russian government to WTO accession was strongly reaffirmed, with the new head of state declaring WTO accession as a goal of his presidency. In turn, the implementation of that commitment has emerged as a key operational objective of Putin's new Ministry of

Economic Development and Trade (MEDT), under the leadership of German Gref. Deputy Minister Maxim Medvedkov has been in charge of the negotiations since the ministry was formed. The accession process has, under this energetic leadership, built up a considerable head of steam. A Draft Working Party Report was published on 28 March 2002. A series of bilateral and multilateral meetings were held through the latter half of 2002, continuing into 2003. The Working Party convened again in February and July 2004. Gref and Medvedkov continue to express confidence that the negotiations can be concluded rapidly, and both the EU and China came out publicly in favour of Russian accession in 2004.[1] It seems, nevertheless, unlikely that accession will be clinched before 2005, and 2007 might be a more realistic prospect.

It is the more difficult to fathom why the process has been so tough in the negotiations, as the overall outcome of Russian accession is almost certain to be positive, if not spectacularly so. Jensen et al. (2002) estimate, on the basis of a calibrated general equilibrium model, that the medium-term gain from accession will amount to 3.2% of GDP. The long-term gain could be 25% of GDP. Those figures suggest that Russian accession should be a routine element in a policy of reintegration into the world economy, one that will provide significant benefits without turning Russia upside down. The true story is clearly much more complex.

Russian accession in the global context: It is tempting to compare Russia's difficult progress with the ease with which other former Soviet countries, namely, Georgia, Kyrgyzstan, Moldova and Armenia, managed to negotiate accession to the WTO, despite their weakness in public administration and limited progress in the general business of transition. But the comparison is not an appropriate one. Georgia, Kyrgyzstan, Moldova and Armenia are small countries, the trade flows of that make little impact on the trading patterns of the majority of existing WTO members. The working parties which determine effectively the outcome of WTO accession negotiations are, furthermore, dominated by major trading countries or blocs like the US and the EU, for which the impact of the accession of a Moldova or a Georgia must seem infinitesimal. Russia, by contrast, like China, is big enough to be a major player in relation to specific trade flows (export of oil; import of food) and specific trading partners (the US and the EU, mainly in relation to agriculture, but also to banking and finance and technology). For that reason, Russia's accession to the WTO is perceived to matter for important domestic commercial interests in major partner countries. Thus, while small former Soviet republics may be 'waved through', the accession of a country like Russia has to be negotiated. The official position in Washington is that the US demands no more, and no less, from Russia than from any other candidate for

1 Russia – WTO: EU-Russia Deal Brings Russia a Step Closer to WTO Membership, http://europa.eu.int/comm/external_relations/russia/intro/ip04_673.htm, 21 May 2004; China Daily, 25 September, 2004.

accession (Bekker & Kaika, 2001). The reality is that in the Russian case, as in the Chinese, Washington (and Brussels) insists on detailed, explicit agreement on many accession issues where a less important candidate would be given the benefit of the doubt. Bilateral negotiations with the EU were concluded in May 2004 (see fn.1), but negotiations with the US continue.

Another dimension on which the comparison between Russia and its smaller erstwhile Soviet partner-republics is inappropriate is that of administrative capacity. Domestic weakness in public administration was not allowed to constrain the accession process for Georgia, Kyrgyzstan, Moldova and Armenia inasmuch as foreign consultants were brought in to handle any aspect of the preparations for accession that was problematic from a technical point of view. There has been technical assistance to the Russian government in relation to WTO accession, but the Russian administration has generally sought to go its way on its own. This stance has brought into sharp relief the deficiencies of capability in the MEDT itself.[2] These deficiencies have undoubtedly slowed up the process of negotiation for accession.

There has also been a geo-strategic dimension to the Russian accession question. Western powers, and in particular the US, have tended to seek to impose forms of conditionality, e.g. in relation to Jewish emigration, which are hangovers from the Cold War era (Hare, 2002, p.6). The revolution in US-Russian relations that has occurred since September 11, has, however, largely removed this kind of impediment to speedy accession. There are still plenty of problems, specifically on the US-Russia axis, but they are essentially economic rather than geo-strategic problems. And they derive essentially from the negotiating stance, or 'offer' of the Russian government.

2 WTO ACCESSION AND RUSSIAN ECONOMIC STRUCTURE AND STRATEGY

Russia is primarily a hydrocarbon producer and exporter. The energy sector (oil, gas, coal and electricity) accounts for some 35% of industrial output and implemented around 63.6% of total industrial investment in the first quarter of 2004. It accounted for nearly 54.7% of recorded exports in the first half of 2004. Russia is the biggest gas exporter in the world and the second-biggest oil exporter. Accession to the WTO will have only a marginal impact on this key sector of the economy, and the energy sector does not figure in the Russian offer. There will certainly be pressure on Russia, in the

2 Interview by author of Evgenii Manakin, deputy director of the Department for Trade Policy and Multilateral Negotiations of the MEDT of the Russian Federation, 28 November 2000.

run-up to accession, to get rid of export taxes on oil and gas.[3] Pressure is already building on Russia to raise domestic energy prices.[4] However, neither of these issues entails WTO-incompatibility as such. There will be pressure, within the context of TRIMs, to ease local-content clauses contained in Production-Sharing Agreements (PSAs) relating to oil and gas. And there will be pressure to allow fair third-party access (TPA) to Russian oil and gas pipelines, for international companies and for other CIS hydrocarbon exporters. But these are not really WTO negotiating points. Access to international oil and gas markets will remain open to Russian exports whatever happens. It would make good sense for the Russian government to rationalise energy prices and ease investment and third-party access regimes in pursuit of its own goals in terms of increasing investment in the fuel and electricity industries. But the WTO is not a key forum for the mediation of energy issues.

Manufacturing accounts for less than 20% of total Russian exports but over 50% of total Russian imports. Russian exports are constrained by the tariffs of other countries, and by various forms of contingent protection. Anti-dumping measures and 'voluntary' export restraints (VERs) have been particularly important in relation to steel and other metals and base chemicals, and in March 2002 Russia was hard hit by the US' imposition of emergency tariffs of up to 30% on all steel imports. While that measure was lifted in December 2003, Russian exports remain subject to 92 restrictive measures imposed by other countries.[5] And import duties have played an important role in limiting imports of specific types of manufactures, with average import tariffs of over 20% on a range of machinery and consumer durable items. The expectation is that these tariffs will have to come down a long way before Russia is allowed into the WTO. In the May 2004 bilateral accord with the EU, Russia agreed that average tariffs on industrial goods should not exceed 7.6%. That means in effect that 7.6% is now the Russian offer on industrial goods - an offer which may, of course, be rejected by other member countries.

The implications of WTO accession for Russian manufacturing are twofold:

- Access for Russian exports of manufactures will be improved.
- Levels of protection for the domestic markets of some Russian manufacturing sectors will be significantly reduced.

The impact under 1., above, would be that much greater if the underlying export capabilities of Russian manufacturing were greater. Thus, the Russian machine-tool

3 The EU has not insisted on this in its bilateral negotiations with Russia. See fn.1

4 In its accord with the EU signed in May 2004 Russia agreed to a gradual increase in domestic gas prices for industrial users to economic levels. See fn.1

5 Pravda, 24 April 2004

industry, a major exporter (admittedly mainly to CMEA markets) in the 1980s, is currently unable to meet minimal specifications for export markets (Gubanov, 2000). In other words, Russia cannot sell machine-tools abroad at any price, under any tariff regime, despite having substantial stocks of human capital in the sector. Some of the sub-sectors where Russia does have a genuine export capability are affected by extra-WTO constraints. One of the few sophisticated manufacturing sectors in which Russia is internationally competitive is space-launching. Russian sources claim that some types of Russian rockets are superior to their American counterparts ('Perspective...', p.13). But the pattern of export of Russian space technology is largely determined by NTBs, notably the relevant clauses of the US-Russian Trade Agreement which imposes sharp limitations on the number of Russian launches of commercial satellites per year (Bzhilianskaya, 1999). It is unlikely that Russian accession to the WTO will have any impact on this. The same can be said in relation to Russian exports of arms (worth $3.6 bn, some 3% of total exports, in 2001[6]) and of nuclear technology. The major constraints here are political, specifically US attempts to stop the export of dangerous technologies to what it perceives to be unfriendly states. In conclusion, the likely short-term impact of WTO accession on Russian exports of manufactures should not be exaggerated. To the extent, however, that Russian government and business seeks to increase exports of conventional manufactures, WTO membership could be an important factor of market access, in terms of lower tariffs and stronger guarantees against anti-dumping actions.

WTO accession could have a significant effect on Russian imports of manufactures in the short term. The Russian motor car industry, which in 1999 enjoyed an average rate of tariff protection of 27.2% (but rising to 80% for some categories of second-hand cars) would not survive WTO accession in its present form on the terms likely to be offered to Russia. The same can be said for the aircraft industry (average rate of tariff protection in 1999 22.9%), and for the clothing, furniture, furnishings and domestic appliances sectors, all of which suffer from generalised problems of poor quality and obsolete design. In 1999 average rates of tariff protection for these latter sectors were, respectively, 27%, 22%, 29.2% and 21.4%. To the extent that these tariffs represent some systematic strategy of import substitution, WTO accession will run directly counter to that strategy. To the extent that liberalisation of imports is perceived as a way of introducing higher standards and more competition into the domestic Russian market, WTO accession will reinforce that strategy.

While some sub-sectors of Russian agriculture enjoy underlying comparative advantage, the food complex of the country is in a parlous state. In 2001 aggregate agricultural output stood at just 40% of the 1990 level. In 2000 the average wheat yield

6 Interview with Sergei Chemezov, first deputy general director of Rosoboronexport (arms exporting company), published in Nezavisimaya Gazeta, 11 December 2001

was 1.48 tons/ha, compared to 6.52 tons/ha for the EU and 2.8 tons/ha for the USA (1997/99 average). The milk yield per milking cow in 1999 was 2356 kg., compared to 5688 kg in the EU and 8043 kg in the US. Around one-half of the large agricultural enterprises were making losses in 2001. With food imports averaging some $10 bn per year, *Russia is one of the biggest agricultural importers in the world*. Russia exports around $2.5-3.0 bn of food products per annum, of which approximately 50% is accounted for by exports of fish and seafood (Moehler, 2001). At first sight, therefore, the main WTO issues for Russian agriculture are on the import side, including access for foreign producers and national food security strategy. But there are potential issues on the export side.

The main problems of Russian agriculture are organisational rather than structural. These problems go back to the Soviet-era, to the imposition of an inefficient system of collective and state farms on the peasantry in the 1930s and the subsequent development of a mentality of passivity amongst the farming population. That system has changed little since transition began in Russia. The collective and state farms have formally been converted into cooperatives, but in reality continue to be controlled by the Soviet-era feudal-bureaucratic stratum of chairmen and managers. Private family farms have been legalised, but agricultural entrepreneurs have struggled to survive in a hostile environment. Private farms account for only about 6% of total agricultural land and the percentage has fallen slightly in recent years. But there has been structural change of a sort in Russian agriculture over the past decade. Soviet agriculture was based on a 'historic compromise', whereby collective and state farmers were allowed to hold and farm 'subsidiary private plots' of around one acre. This provided subsistence, and also allowed the peasants a small cash income from the sale of, for example, eggs. At the same time it reinforced attitudes of passivity vis-à-vis the collective and state farms. At the end of the Soviet period the private plots were accounting for some 25-30% of total agricultural output. Under transition the plots have flourished, accounting currently for an extraordinary 60% of total agricultural production. Formal and informal leasing arrangements with the big farms have allowed the private plots to increase their aggregate share of total agricultural area from around 4% to over 20%. But this triumph of the principle of private enterprise is more apparent than real. The price of success in the subsidiary private sector is apathy and failure in the collective/cooperative sector. Farmers in their subsidiary private capacity pay no tax. And the private plots benefit from subsidised inputs, notably fertilisers, and credit extended by the government to the big farms. To an extent, the profits of the private subsidiary sector derive from the losses of the cooperative sector, with the latter being 'hollowed out' through transfer of assets to the former. If all these organisational problems could be resolved, Russia re-emerged well as a significant agricultural exporter.

In the May 2004 bilateral accord with the EU, Russia agreed to a maximum average tariff of 13% on agricultural goods and 11% on fishery products. These figures now effectively represent the Russian offer on food.

The Russian banking and insurance sectors are extremely weak. There are currently some 1,300 banks in Russia. But many of these are insolvent, and many are not proper banks in that they do not offer comprehensive lending and clearing facilities to clients. Total bank deposits in Russia represented 18.6% of GDP in 2000, compared to 63% in OECD countries and 33.8 in Poland, which can perhaps be taken as a yardstick transition economy. Loans by banks represent only 12% of GDP, compared to around 45% in OECD countries. The Russian banking system was badly hit by the August 1998 crisis, and total bank assets on 1 January 2001 stood at just 90% of the pre-crisis level, with a corresponding figure for capital of 85%. The situation is similar in the insurance sector. At the beginning of 2001 there were 1,170 insurance companies. Russian insurance is, however, dominated by ten (relatively) big companies, which account for 42% of total gross premia. The top 100 firms account for 89% of that total. At present total insurance premia (Rb276.6bn - $8.7bn - in 2001) represent around 2% of GDP. The corresponding figure for the EU for general insurance alone is 7%. Total premia collected was 62% higher in 2001 than in 2000 (Fickett, 2003). It is estimated that removal of non-tariff barriers affecting financial services in Russia would reduce the prices of such services by 21-28% (Zemnitskii, 2002, p.4).

The Russian banking and insurance sectors are protected by quite explicit non-tariff barriers. In the aggregate foreign banks are limited to 12% of total bank capital. The corresponding figure for insurance appears to have been raised from 15% to 25% in 2003 or 2004. These and other restrictions reflect a clear commitment by the Russian government to protect the domestic financial sector. It is not clear, however, that this protectionist commitment makes a huge difference in practice. The limits on foreign capital in the banking and insurance sectors have, in fact, never been reached. In 2000 foreign banks accounted for just 4.9% of total banking assets in Russia, with a corresponding figure for the insurance sector of 4.0%. By the beginning of 2001 the figure for banking had risen to 7.7%, though by April 2001 it had fallen back to 6.1%, on account of growth in the capitalisation of Russian banks.[7] Even so, Russia is under strong pressure from existing WTO members to relax these restrictions.

For the banking sector, the Russian government originally proposed the following restrictions on the activity of foreign banks:

- Aggregate foreign participation in the Russian banking sector to be limited to a maximum of 25% of total capital
- Minimum charter capital for a new, foreign bank to be set at €10 m.
- Foreign banks to be allowed to take deposits from private individuals only from two years after registration

7 http://www.regions.ru, 18 June, 2002

For insurance, the proposed restrictions are:

- Aggregate foreign participation in the Russian insurance sector to be limited to a maximum of 25% of total capital
- Up to 2007, insurance companies for which the extent of foreign ownership exceeds 49% must have minimum charter capital of ten times the corresponding minimum for Russian-owned companies.
- The foreign owner of a Russian insurance company must have been selling non-life insurance for 15 years in its domestic market, and participating in the Russian market for two years, before it can sell non-life insurance in Russia.

The tenor of these restrictions is palpably discriminatory, those which relate to insurance marginally more so than those relating to banking.

In relation to intellectual property rights (IPRs), Russia finds itself in a delicate situation. Though there was a certain amount of Soviet patenting in the US, and a good deal of licensing of foreign technologies to Soviet organisations, the Soviet Union remained largely outside the international IPR system. There was systematic industrial espionage in the West, and a substantial proportion of the Western technology used in Soviet enterprises was pirated. Over the years of transition, the situation has been complicated rather than regularised. A new wave of piracy, centred mainly on software products, has washed over the Russian economy. Thus, it is estimated that in Russia *alone US companies lost $1 bn from video piracy in 2000* (Hare, 2002, p.13). The Russian Office of Economic Security estimates that in 2000 the share of counterfeit titles in the Russian video market reached 50%. The corresponding figure for CDs and tapes is 64%, and for counterfeit industrial and consumer goods 10-50%.

At the same time, the scope for direct inter-company trade in IPRs and human capital that transition has opened up, has raised for the first time, the issue of violation of Russian IPRs abroad. Accession to the WTO, specifically to TRIPs, would raise serious issues in relation to unauthorised use of foreign technologies within the Russian domestic economy. We should not, however, exaggerate how critical these issues might be. Russian factories and warehouses are certainly full of 'me-too' products and processes, but in many cases it would be difficult to establish the IPRs over these products and processes in a court of law. It must be stressed, too, that Russian government policy is evolving here, independent of WTO accession issues, and for good public health reasons. The Russian health ministry for example is waging a campaign against pirated (and often dangerous) medicines.

With all these qualifications, accession to TRIPs could still cost Russia a lot in the short term, in terms of making peace with major international IPR holders. The advantage for Russia is, again, in the longer term. If we accept the Zysman argument that IPRs lie at the heart of contemporary international production networks (IPNs) (Borrus & Zysman, 1997), then we must accept that effective international technology transfer requires inclusion within global IPR networks. By the same token, accession to TRIPS will afford

Russian companies real advantages in terms of turning their own IPRs to account. And it would make it easier for the Russian authorities to structure their efforts to re-educate their businessmen in this respect.

3 INTERPRETING THE STRATEGY - RESIDUAL STATE CAPITALISM OR GIVING IN TO THE LOBBIES?

That industrial and regional lobbies are in general very powerful within the Russian polity and that Russian manufacturing is in some general sense protectionist is well attested (Hanson, 1997; Dyker, 2000; Fry, 2002). That nationalistic and étatist views are strongly represented among political and administrative elites can be read, for example, from the records of the debates of the State Duma. That the negotiating stance of the Russian government vis-à-vis accession to the WTO is the product of the resolution of the tension between these two political fields can hardly be disputed as a general proposition. But in Russia there are liberal as well as protectionist lobbies. And while the mind-set of the Russian political elites may be generally nationalistic and conservative, there are big generational differences, and big differences between departments of the state administration. There can be no doubt that Mr Medvedkov, who is in charge of those negotiations on a day-to-day basis, is strongly committed to accession. That does not mean that he is against the use of trade policy for purposes of industrial policy. So configurations are complex. To make clearer sense of them, we need to look at some individual case material.

Agriculture: While individual agriculturalists often take up extreme protectionist positions, the position of leading lobbyists is relatively nuanced. Thus Ivan Starikov, chairman of the food and agriculture committee of the Federation Council (upper house of parliament) sees infrastructural investment and increasing the purchasing power of the Russian population as the keys to the long-term development of Russian agriculture. Because incomes in Russia will rise only slowly, however, it is imperative, Starikov argues, to develop exports, with the emphasis on ecologically pure products ('Rossiiskii agroprom...', 2002). If Starikov were in charge of the WTO negotiations, one might expect a tough but flexible approach. In practice, in mid-2004, the negotiating position of the Russian government on agriculture remained tough and inflexible in relation to tariffs and export subsidies, and still a major obstacle to general progress on accession. One can only speculate that considerations of state policy, in this case perhaps primarily focused on national security, have been to the fore in defining the Russian negotiating position. The Russian government wants to keep its options open in relation to agriculture and that means sticking out for a level of protection which, in truth, the Russian budget could not afford. Whether we look at internal or external evidence, however, there is no compelling argument that the agricultural lobby has played a critical role in forming the Russian negotiating position on agriculture.

Motor cars: The Russian motor-car producers' lobby has waged a sustained campaign in favour of higher duties on imported cars, especially second-hand ones. Specifically, they have demanded an increase in the duty on imported new cars from 25% to 35%, and substantial increases on tariffs on imported second-hand cars more than seven years old (Simakov & Miledin, 2002; Smirnov, 2002). The Russian government has taken a firm, but nuanced line with the industry over these demands. On the one hand, it has held its position on keeping import tariffs on new cars and cars under seven years old unchanged. On the other hand it has shown a willingness to trade concessions on tariffs on cars over seven years old for commitments on the part of the domestic industry to come into line with Euro-4 standards for the industry by 2010. In particular, it wants electronic regulation of engines in every Russian car. In 2002, no Russian car had this feature (Simakov & Miledin, 2002). The position of the Russian government on protection for the car industry has, however, been complicated by President Putin's personal interest in the matter. In 2002, the President accused the government of 'lacking the guts to implement a policy of defending national producers, particularly in the car industry' (Simakov & Miledin, 2002). The upshot of all this is that the government now seems prepared to make further concessions to the industry on imported cars more than seven years old, but remains inflexible on tariffs on other categories of imported cars.

Banking and insurance: In the past, the financial services sector has witnessed some of the most powerful and sustained lobbying by interested parties.[8] In the last couple of years, however, there has been a fairly dramatic change. In June 2002, Aleksandr Koval, president of the All-Russia Union of Insurers, announced that Russian insurance companies would no longer oppose the granting of free access to foreign insurers on the grounds that foreign insurance companies that really wanted to penetrate the Russian market were in any case able to circumvent the restrictions.[9] The shift in stance on the part of the insurers may in part reflect a realisation that not every Western insurance company will want to fish in Russian waters. It also reflects a growing confidence on the part of the Russian industry in its ability to exploit its 'insider' advantages and withstand the competition (Shokhina, 2004). In more concrete terms, it seems that behind the change lies a deal between government and lobby. The deal involves a number of concessions to the insurers, notably tax concessions in relation to life insurance policies. All of this demonstrates clearly that in this case it is, or was, the sectoral lobby rather than the government that was driving the opposition to WTO requirements. It also, however, raises further questions. Will the concessions given to

8 See Assotsiyatsiya Rossiiskikh Bankov (Association of Russian Banks), Kontseptual'nye Osnovy Razvitiya Bankovskoi Sistemy Rossii (Conceptual Bases for the Development of the Banking System of Russia), May 2000, www.arb.ru/page.php?id=2&d_id=1, Section 8

9 Vedomosti, 14 June 2002

the Russian insurers generate secondary level-playing field problems? It is impossible on the basis of available information to answer this question.

These striking changes in the attitudes of the Russian insurance companies have not been paralleled in the banking sector. At around the same time as Koval was making his path-breaking announcement, a number of leading Russian bankers publicly reiterated their established position, viz. that the Russian banking system is not competitive, and that free access for foreign banks would leave Russia at the mercy of foreign banks.[10] The powerful Association of Russian Banks (ARB) has proposed that the limit on foreign participation should be set at 15% rather than 25%, with the possibility of raising it to 25% later on.[11] Here, as (formerly) in the insurance case, it is clear that the pressure for protectionism comes from the lobby rather than the government. It is equally clear, however, that the government believes that totally free access to foreign banks would effectively give a privileged position to foreign banks, and would accelerate the rate of capital flight.[12] And banking is one of the sectors in which the EU has been persuaded to accept significant continued restrictions.[13] In all of this, the interests of the clients of Russian banks seem to carry the least weight of all.

4 CONCLUSIONS

Russian policy on WTO accession clearly reflects elements of residual state capitalism, but the imprint of a few powerful sectoral lobbies is also plain to see. Just as different elements within the state have different attitudes to protection and free trade in general, however, those different elements have taken up opposing positions on specific issues relating to the offer. Thus, the general stance of Russian policy does, indeed, encompass elements of infant industry strategy and trade liberalisation as an instrument of domestic reform strategy. There is no evidence whatsoever of the Russian government taking a liberal stance on a particular issue in the name of protection of consumer interests. On the industry side, the lobbies are anything, but immovable objects. As we saw in the case of insurance, they can change their strategies quickly enough in response to perceived changes in circumstances. One thing is clear. If the governments and technical assistance activists of the developed industrial countries want to influence the Russian offer, they will need to adopt a multi-

10 http://www.regions.ru, 18 June, 2002

11 Pravda, 18 June 2002

12 Izvestiya, 25 July 2002

13 See fn.1

level approach. It is not enough to talk to the Russian government, much less to just the part of that government to which the WTO negotiations are entrusted. Finally, in looking at the problem of agriculture, which the Russian State finds most inflexible, the European Commission and US government might reflect that exactly the same is true for themselves. In traversing the long and difficult road to Russian WTO accession, the global trading community may yet hope that the end result will be a better and fairer system for all.

References

Bekker, A., Kaika, Z. (2001), 'Robert Zellik: Rossiyu primut v VTO na obshchikh usloviyakh', Vedomosti, 3 October 2001, p.A5 (Interview with US representative on WTO Russia Working Party Robert Zoellick)

Borrus, M. & Zysman, J. (1997), 'Globalisation with borders: the rise of Wintelism as the future of industrial competition', in eds. J.Zysman & A.Schwartz, Enlarging Europe: the Industrial Foundations of a New Political Reality, Berkeley, University of California

Bzhilianskaya, L. (1999), 'Foreign direct investment in the science-based industries of Russia', in ed. D.A.Dyker, Foreign Direct Investment and Technology Transfer in the Former Soviet Union, Edward Elgar, Cheltenham

Dyker, D. A. (2000), 'The structural origins of the Russian economic crisis', Post-Communist Economies, vol.12, No.1, pp.5-24

Dyker, D. A. (2001), 'Technology exchange and the foreign business sector in Russia', Research Policy, vol.30, pp.851-68

Dyker, D. A. (2002), 'Making sense of post-Soviet economic space - free trade and beyond in the CIS', Ritsumeikan Economic Review, vol.51, No.1, April, pp.43-56

Fickett, L.P. (2003), 'The Russian evolution', Risk Transfer, vol.1, No.3, 25 February

Fry, T. (2002), 'Capture or exchange? Business lobbying in Russia', Europe-Asia Studies, vol.54, No.7, pp.1017-1036, November

Gubanov, S., (2000), 'Stankostroenie: usloviya konkurentosposobnosti', Ekonomist, No.9

Hanson, P. (1997), 'What sort of capitalism is developing in Russia?', Communist Economies and Economic Transformation, vol.9, No.1, pp.27-42

Hare, P. (2002), Russia and the World Trade Organisation, mimeo, School of Management, Heriot-Watt University, May

Jensen, S.E.H., Rutherford, T.F. & Tarr, D. (2002), 'Economy-wide effects of Russia's accession to the WTO', CEFIR (Moscow) (www.cefir.ru)

Moehler, R. (2001), Accession of Russia to the World Trade Organisation. The Implications for Russian Agriculture, DFID

'Perspektivy rossiiskoi kosmonavtiki i naukoemkikh tekhnologii' (2000), Ekonomist, No.8

Shokhina, E. (2004), 'Two-thirds of the way there', Gateway to Russia, 31 May

Simakov, D. & Miledin, P. (2002), 'Inomarki poshchadili: Kas'yanov ne poshel na povodu u avtopromyshlennikov', Vedomosti, 19 August

Smirnov, K. (2002), 'Poderzhannye inomarki dorozhayut', Kommersant, 13 August

Zemnitskii, A.V. (2002) 'Otsenka posledstvii ustraneniya netarifnykh bar'yerov dlya inostrannykh kompanii v sektore uslug rossiiskoi ekonomiki: strukturnyi podkhod', CEFIR (Moscow) (www.cefir.ru)

LE TERRORISME TRANSNATIONAL ET LA POLITISATION DE LA PEUR

Réflexions théoriques sur la stratégie terroriste et sur la politique anti-terroriste de l'Union Européenne, de la Russie et des Etats Unis

ANDREAS VASILACHE

1 INTRODUCTION

Dire que la peur règne est, dans beaucoup de langues indo-européennes, une expression assez fréquente.[1] Dans ce syntagme le règne, mot-clé politique est mis en relation avec un état émotionnel (la peur). Il est peu probable que cette construction verbale soit le résultat d'une coïncidence étonnante. On pourrait l'expliquer par le fait que la peur, état affectif de base,[2] peut atteindre une telle intensité que l'individu se sente saisi et »gouverné« par elle. Malgré cette explication psychologique possible, une réflexion politologique du rapport entre le domaine du pouvoir politique et l'émotion, la peur, nous paraît nécessaire. Car bien que le rapprochement de ces termes si différents dans le langage courant ne constitue pas forcément la preuve d'un lien inhérent entre les deux sphères, il paraît néanmoins dans notre cas qu'une corrélation entre la peur et la domination, c'est à dire entre la peur et la politique, existe.

On a parlé du rôle de la peur dans la politique spécialement dans le cadre de la recherche sur le totalitarisme, et on a reconnu la terreur d'Etat comme élément nécessaire sinon comme élément constitutif des systèmes totalitaires.[3] Par la répression vers l'intérieur l'Etat totalitaire a l'intention de créer une atmosphère de peur qui empêche des éventuels mouvements d'opposition, qui ait un effet paralysant sur la société et qui assure ainsi le pouvoir du gouvernement. Cette thèse a bien sûr souvent été disputée et combattue dans les discussions théoriques. La philosophe Hannah Arendt démontre qu'il faut différencier entre pouvoir et violence et qu'un régime

1 Pour autant que je puisse en juger, c'est le cas non seulement pour les langues germaniques et romanes, mais encore pour les langues slaves.

2 Voir Putz-Osterloh (2000: 1).

3 Voir Neumann (1954: 34, 42 et suivantes) et pour les controverses sur le totalitarisme l'anthologie de Jesse (1996).

totalitaire fondé sur la violence ne pourrait pas subsister à long terme sans un certain consensus.[4] Dans le domaine des relations internationales, le rapport entre la peur et la politique a joué un rôle, surtout dans la discussion sur le confit Est-Ouest et sur la course aux armements. Ce qu'on a appelé équilibre de la peur entre l'OTAN et le Pacte de Varsovie a été considéré par les uns comme une menace[5] tandis que les autres voyaient en lui un élément pacificateur.[6] Mais exactement comme dans la recherche sur le totalitarisme, la relation entre la peur et la politique a été considérée seulement comme un détail particulier des relations internationales. En général, on a accordé peu d'attention à la relation entre la peur et la politique dans les sciences politiques. Au vu des conflits qui - comme dans la situation de la lutte contre le terrorisme - sont souvent trop vite présentés et publiquement interprétés comme des conflits globaux, il est important de réfléchir sur le rôle de la peur dans la politique d'une manière fondamentale.

Même si dans l'analyse qui suit, le rôle de la peur dans la politique internationale reste le centre de la discussion, la sphère intérieure des Etats ne sera pas exclue. Mais à la différence de la recherche sur le totalitarisme, où le rôle politique de la peur a été thématisé surtout eu égard à la politique intérieure, nous voulons parler surtout des implications internationales de la peur qui existe au niveau de l'Etat. Dans le cadre de la lutte contre le terrorisme il faut discuter du rôle joué par la peur vue comme une motivation et comme un pouvoir politique créateur et légitimateur. Il faut se demander également si la théorie moderne des relations internationales ne devrait pas tenir compte de la peur et l'apprécier comme puissance et paramètre central. Au cours de cette argumentation on va se demander aussi s'il est possible de considérer la peur comme une ressource politique qui pourrait ouvrir et réguler de nouvelles marges de manœuvre. Le terme de ressource implique une certaine disponibilité et maniabilité politique de la peur et surtout son caractère instrumental.

Il faut faire mention d'une restriction que nous allons faire dans la discussion suivante. Même si la peur comme émotion opère surtout sur l'individu, il ne s'agit pas ici d'expliquer la naissance de la peur individuelle suite aux actions politiques. Notre intérêt ne se dirige pas vers la psychologie individuelle de la peur mais plutôt vers les implications politiques d'un état émotionnel collectif.

4 Voir Arendt (1994: 36-58).

5 Voir par exemple Czempiel (1999: 76, 82).

6 Voir par exemple Bergsdorf (2000: 21).

2 REFLEXIONS THEORIQUES

Les puissances impérialistes classiques ont dû considérer la peur de leurs peuples d'une façon sceptique. Car même si aux yeux du gouvernement une certaine peur - produite par la violence du régime - paraît avoir un effet stabilisateur, la peur doit être considérée pourtant comme le pire des ennemis d'une politique militaire expansionniste. Si on examine l'Empire Romain, l'Empire Ottoman, l'Empire Mongol ou bien les croisades, on voit qu'une politique militaire impériale et expansionniste n'est pas réalisable dans des conditions sociales de peur. Certes, le soldat, seul devant l'ennemi, aura peur de mourir, mais le moral collectif de la population doit être animé par la confiance, l'optimisme et l'espérance - bien sûr indépendamment de la question de savoir si ce climat émotionnel public soit justifié et légitime ou pas. Car la peur a un effet paralysant et, par là, réduit la volonté ainsi que le potentiel d'une politique expansionniste militaire. Donc d'un point de vue politique, la peur était un état d'esprit nuisible et dangereux qu'il fallait combattre par une confiance optimiste el un courage héroïque. Une puissance impériale ne peut pas accepter la peur, ni celle de son peuple en ce qui concerne l'expansion dans des nouveaux territoires, ni la peur de l'empire face aux autres empires.

Dans l'histoire moderne, lors de la Révolution française on a codifié pour la première fois la propre peur de l'Etat vis-à-vis d'autres puissances. Puisque la Révolution fut légitimée au nom des droits universels de l'homme et du citoyen, on pouvait supposer que la France voulait prolonger la lutte contre la monarchie, au-delà de ses frontières. Mais par le postulat de la souveraineté nationale, la République française assurait, qu'en dépit de la validité universelle de ses valeurs, elle ne voulait pas s'ingérer dans les affaires des monarchies et des principautés voisines. Par cela la France ne voulait pas seulement confirmer la souveraineté de ces principautés mais elle voulait surtout s'assurer que les voisins n'aillent pas s'ingérer dans ses propres affaires.[7] Ainsi le principe de non-ingérence peut être interprété comme une forme de traitement de sa propre peur; une forme encore jeune et par conséquent ambivalente et en sus cachée. La peur de la France face à l'immixtion étrangère est thématisée comme la peur des pays voisins envers la France. Le principe général de non-ingérence qui devait servir la France elle-même sera introduit comme une restriction bénévole et généreuse de la France qui promet de ne pas déranger les monarchies voisines, en dépit du fondement universel des valeurs républicaines.

Que le thème de la peur dans la politique et spécialement dans les relations internationales soit étroitement lié à la question de la souveraineté moderne se laisse démontrer aussi par le fondement théorique des Etats constitutionnels modernes. A l'époque moderne, le philosophe et penseur contractualiste anglais Thomas Hobbes

7 Voir Seidelmann (1998: 134).

peut être considéré comme le plus important théoricien de la peur. Dans son Leviathan, il caractérise la peur de la mort[8] comme un trait caractéristique de l'être humain qui transforme les hommes en créatures paisibles. Cette peur de mourir poussa les hommes à sortir de leur état de nature guerrier et menaçant, et à se soumettre à la législation générale. Selon Hobbes, la liberté naturelle des hommes mène inévitablement à la guerre de chacun contre chacun.[9] La peur des hommes d'être blessés ou même tués mène en conséquence à la ratification d'un contrat qui conduit à la soumission et à la perte de leur liberté naturelle face à un souverain. Ce processus marque la constitution et la création de l'Etat. Dans la mythologie de l'origine des sociétés modernes, Hobbes attribue à la peur le rôle motivant dans la constitution de l'Etat. Nous pouvons finalement conclure que la peur obtient le statut d'une force morale.

L'anthropologie pessimiste de Thomas Hobbes et l'image qu'il a de l'état de nature qui se présente comme une guerre perpétuelle, constituent les bases philosophiques de l'école de pensée réaliste des relations internationales et influencent dans une mesure assez importante la pratique de la politique. Mais avec le dépassement de l'état de nature par les individus et avec la création de l'Etat national, l'état de nature ne cesse pas d'exister. Il sera seulement transféré du niveau interpersonnel au niveau international.[10] Dans les relations entre les Etats, c'est-à-dire dans le système international, il règne un danger permanent de conflits guerriers car les Etats - comme auparavant les hommes - ne répondent pas de leurs actions devant aucune puissance supérieure. Et tout comme dans l'état de nature des individus, dans le système international c'est la loi du plus fort qui détermine le sort des sujets, qui maintenant, ne sont pas les individus mais les Etats.

Ce (dés-) ordre anarchique du système international se présente pour les Etats comme une menace permanente, car ils ne peuvent être jamais sûrs de la paix. Et puisque même le comportement pacifique d'un Etat dans une telle structure internationale est interprété comme une faiblesse chaque Etat aura la tendance d'augmenter son potentiel militaire. Cette menace structurelle crée entre les Etats une atmosphère de méfiance et de peur qui est structurellement équivalente à la peur de la mort des individus à l'état de nature. La méfiance et la peur ne caractérisent donc plus la relation entre les individus mais la celle entre les Etats.

Dans le cadre des conflits internationaux classiques, ce modèle peut bien sûr livrer un certain potentiel d'explications. Néanmoins ce modèle n'est pas seulement centré sur la nation et l'Etat, mais ce modèle est plutôt limité à un point de vue étatique. En dépit

8 Voir Hobbes (1998: 98).

9 Voir ibid.: 96.

10 Voir ibid.: 269 et suivante.

de cette analogie convaincante entre l'état de nature interpersonnel et l'état de nature international, le potentiel explicatif de ce modèle est de peu de valeur si on veut discuter et analyser le phénomène du terrorisme transnational. Car dans la situation du terrorisme transnational, les sujets qui agissent ne sont pas forcément des Etats. Ainsi dans le cas du terrorisme, la peur ne peut être réduite à la peur d'un Etat vis-à-vis d'un autre Etat. Dans le chapitre suivant nous allons analyser la relation et le rapport entre la peur et la politique eu égard au terrorisme transnational et démontrer les implication de ce rapport pour la théorie des relations internationales.

3 LE TERRORISME

Déjà ce bref résumé de la théorie du contrat de Hobbes démontre sa détermination et sa fixation étatique. Mais le terrorisme transnational n'est pas explicable d'une manière adéquate à l'aide d'un vocabulaire limité à un point de vue national et étatique. Ainsi le terme courant de »terrorisme international« est déroutant, car le terrorisme n'est pas une stratégie habituelle d'un Etat contre un autre Etat, mais bien un phénomène transnational qui agit donc au travers des Etats et au-delà de leurs frontières. Et même au cas où ce sont les Etats qui commandent l'action terroriste, cela se passe en secret, l'action ne se dirigeant pas directement contre un autre Etat mais contre des cibles civiles.[11] En général les stratégies terroristes sont poursuivies par des petites factions avec une motivation nationale, ethnique, religieuse ou politique, qui, à travers des attaques spectaculaires, veulent attirer l'attention sur leurs objectifs politiques, effrayer l'adversaire et éveiller la sympathie de leur propre communauté nationale, ethnique ou religieuse.[12] Même si les Etats peuvent bien sûr constituer des cibles pour les terroristes, les cibles concrètes de l'attaque ne sont pas obligatoirement les équipements ou les institutions publics. C'est pourquoi pour les terroristes, les frontières des Etats ne représentent pas des barrières politiques d'importance. Pour la stratégie terroriste, le lieu de l'attaque n'est pas essentiel. Du point de vue stratégique des groupes terroristes, cela ne fait aucune différence s'ils s'attaquent à une boite de nuit de Bali, à une discothèque de Berlin, à un avion, au métro ou au théâtre de Moscou, aux synagogues en Tunisie on en Turquie ou au World Trade Center. Du point de vue de ceux qui sont menacés par des actions terroristes, les attaques à l'intérieur du propre pays ont bien sûr un effet encore beaucoup plus menaçant. Mais puisque les terroristes ne poursuivent pas une lutte territoriale classique, les attaques

11 Des exemples de terrorisme d'Etat sont l'attentat contre l'avion de la Pan-Am qui s'écrasa en 1988 sur Lockerbie et l'attaque terroriste de la discothèque La Belle à Berlin, attribués à la police secrète de Libye.

12 Voir Waldmann (1998: 10).

sur le propre territoire ne peuvent pas être interprétées comme une escalade du conflit, mais représentent seulement une intensification quantitative des effets psychologiques de l'intimidation. Par les attentats et les attaques - qui font peur et intimident la population - les terroristes veulent placer leurs sujets et leurs objectifs dans les discussions politiques et mettre la balle dans le camp de l'adversaire.

Même si l'on attribue au terrorisme qui opère sur la base de nombreux petits groupes clandestins, bien cachés et inaperçus, une grande puissance conspiratrice, la brutalité et l'arbitraire de la stratégie terroriste est plutôt le résultat de la faiblesse des groupes terroristes et de l'absence d'une base de pouvoir stable. Les organisations terroristes sont trop faibles pour affronter leurs trop forts adversaires d'une manière directe et par des stratégies et des moyens conventionnels. Pour quand même attirer l'attention de l'opinion publique, ils recourent à l'arbitraire et à la brutalité.[13] La logique des attaques doit annoncer que jusqu'à l'obtention de leurs buts politiques, aucun citoyen du camp adverse ne sera plus en sûreté, fût-il à la maison, sur son lieu de travail, en voyage, dans les moyens de transport, dans son pays ou à l'étranger. Le terrorisme, stratégie qui est non-territoriale et transnationale est surtout une stratégie psychologique et communicative de la peur.

En fait, le terrorisme transnational réussit à semer la peur et la terreur. Parfois, la peur du terrorisme dans la population est beaucoup plus forte que la menace réelle.[14] Voire par exemple l'achat massif de masques à gaz et de kits de survie depuis le 11.09.01 aux Etats Unis. Et aussi l'installation d'abris dans des maisons d'habitation et la demande de véhicules blindés ou de type militaire ainsi que les réactions dans le domaine du tourisme attestent de la peur de la population américaine.

On peut conclure que la peur doit être considérée comme ressource centrale des stratégies terroristes. Provoquer la peur et la terreur reste, à cause de leur faiblesse, la seule possibilité d'agir et le seul potentiel des associations terroristes. Vu le fait qu'à la différence des conflits militaires traditionnels il y a peu de victimes, l'assassinat des personnes civiles, et/ou des personnes importantes ne suit pas une stratégie conventionnelle. Au centre des attaques, il y a le but de générer la peur. La systématique de cette production révèle en plus le caractère de ressource de la peur dans la politique terroriste. La génération de la peur est le but stratégique central qui, bien planifié et calculé, sera atteint grâce aux attaques. Dans la provocation de la peur, les terroristes comptent en plus sur le pouvoir multiplicateur des médias.[15]

[13] Voir ibid.: 10 et suivantes, 15, 19 et Hoffman (2002: 51, 56).

[14] Voir par exemple Hoffman (2002: 197 et suivantes) qui démontre ce phénomène par des sondages américains.

[15] Pour le rôle des médias dans le discours de la peur voir – même si c'est de manière un peu indifférenciée – Bergsdorf (2000: 23 et suivantes).

A la stratégie de la production de peur, qui peut être considérée comme illimitée, sans frontières ou, employons un terme moderne, globalisée, correspond structurellement la réaction des éventuelles victimes civiles. La peur des attaques terroristes est confuse et omniprésente. Tandis que la crainte de quelque chose a des traits concrets et que l'élément qui la produit peut être défini,[16] la peur du terrorisme, à cause de son omniprésence virtuelle, ne dépendant ni d'endroit, ni d'heure ni de situation, par conséquent reste vague et confuse. Et pareillement à la stratégie terroriste qui ne tient pas compte des frontières, la peur des groupes menacés par le terrorisme se globalise à son tour. Dans le cas du terrorisme ce n'est pas un Etat national qui a peur d'un autre, mais c'est la peur des individus, des groupes ou des Etats vis-à-vis des acteurs transnationaux organisés et interconnectés au-delà des frontières. Puisque la peur n'est pas ciblée et ne vise aucune personne concrète, il y a le risque d'être soupçonné trop vite de sympathiser avec le terrorisme. Dans le cas du terrorisme islamiste, ce ne sont pas seulement des pays comme l'Iran ou la Libye qui font l'objet de critique, mais en même temps il y a la tendance de suspecter - parfois en bloc - les musulmans qui vivent dans un pays occidental et qui souvent sont déjà naturalisés.[17]

Comme on l'a déjà vu, la violence terroriste, par son caractère illimité et par la globalisation de la peur qu'elle provoque, est largement incompatible avec le concept étatiste de Hobbes. Mais même si l'étatisme théorique de Hobbes ne peut expliquer suffisamment le terrorisme transnational, il y a quand même un point central dans ses idées qui peut servir à comprendre le terrorisme moderne. Le terrorisme est ainsi - comme nous l'avons déjà montré - surtout une stratégie politico-psychologique de la peur. Et c'est justement la peur qui dans l'anthropologie de Thomas Hobbes, joue le rôle d'une force politique centrale. La différence consiste dans le fait que la peur, dans le système international règne entre les Etats, tandis que dans des circonstances transnationales, elle saisit à nouveau l'individu. Le terrorisme transnational peut être interprété comme l'activation du climat de peur décrit par Hobbes dans les conditions de la gouvernementalité moderne,[18] c'est-à-dire dans les conditions de la politique moderne qui agit par et se base sur des réseaux complexes. C'est notamment le philosophe français Michel Foucault qui a démontré comment le pouvoir est (re-)

16 La distinction conceptuelle entre la peur et la crainte provient du philosophe danois Sören Kierkegaard (1912: 36 et suivante).

17 Que la discussion de la cohabitation de cultures différentes dans les sociétés occidentales et surtout le dialogue avec l'islam ait acquis, depuis le 11.09.01, une autre complexité, se reflète aussi dans le fait que dans les discussions sur le multiculturalisme, le thème du terrorisme doit toujours être pris en compte.

18 Pour la notion et le concept de la gouvernementalité voir Lemke (2003: 267, 269 et suivantes) qui reformule, modifie et transforme des conceptions foucaultiennes et par là les rend productives pour l'analyse politique.

produit et exercé dans des réseaux décentralisés complexes.[19] La conception de Foucault sur la production et l'exercice discursif du pouvoir ne fonctionne pas d'une façon hiérarchique, mais le pouvoir agit dans une combinaison compliquée de différentes autorités et institutions qu'on pourrait définir comme nœuds centraux d'un réseau. Dans un pareil réseau, les auteurs des actions politiques ne sont pas centralisés dans un endroit (par exemple dans un pays ou dans un gouvernement) et par conséquent il est difficile de les localiser et de les fixer. Dans un tel réseau on communique par des pratiques discursives qui fonctionnent selon des règles définies et des critères d'exclusion.[20]

Il nous semble que le terrorisme transnational peut donc être caractérisé par ce modèle. D'un côté la stratégie terroriste est marquée par la primauté de la peur. La provocation de la peur et de l'effroi est son trait principal. Si le terrorisme veut mettre en valeur son potentiel de peur, il faudra d'autre part éveiller chez son adversaire un sentiment d'insécurité, d'incertitude et de confusion. Le caractère de réseau du terrorisme n'est donc pas né exclusivement des circonstances pratiques, il n'est pas seulement dû au fait que les terroristes sont obligés d'opérer en secret et de rester dans l'ombre. Le terrorisme réussit à propager son effroi plutôt dans des situations de grande confusion et d'incertitude. A l'exemple du terrorisme islamiste transnational, on peut constater que, vu le nombre immense de cibles potentielles et l'imprévisibilité de la prochaine attaque, le sentiment de menace, ainsi que l'importance politique de cette forme de terrorisme s'intensifient et augmentent. A la différence des mouvements terroristes clairement identifiés, comme l'ETA, l'IRA ou le RAF, ce qu'on appelle le terrorisme islamiste est un réseau complexe et hétérogène.[21] Ce réseau est si diversifié qu'il peut réunir des membres d'un gouvernement ou de la police secrète d'un Etat, des chefs religieux, des musulmans de l'extrême droite, tout comme des hommes d'affaires arabes ou des prédicateurs de petites communautés dans la diaspora. En plus, on peut seulement supposer la dimension et l'intensité de l'organisation et de l'interconnexion dans ce réseau islamiste. La cohésion de ce réseau est obtenue par un discours extrémiste, construit sur le fondement théorique d'idées religieuses imprécises et confuses, et autour des intérêts ou ennemis communs. En fait, ce discours ne doit pas être considéré comme une communication directe au sein d'une structure organisée et bien définie. Il s'agit plutôt de la transmission désordonnée de signes les plus différents, qui vont depuis une vidéo d'El Keida jusqu'aux paroles anti-sémites des jeunes musulmans. Ce discours décentralisé

19 Voir par exemple Foucault (1975: 227; 1998: 15, 36 et suivante, 59, 92 et suivante, 106 et suivantes).

20 Voir à ce sujet Vasilache (2003: 46; 2005).

21 Voir aussi Heine (2001: 154).

qui n'est pas dirigé garantit ainsi la présentation de l'extrémisme islamiste vers l'intérieur et l'extérieur.

Après avoir présenté le terrorisme transnational comme une stratégie de la peur dans les conditions d'une gouvernementalité moderne, dans le chapitre suivant, nous allons analyser la politisation de la peur dans les réactions des groupes et des Etats menacés par le terrorisme. Au centre de notre discussion nous allons placer les Etats constitutionnels d'Europe, ainsi que ceux d'Amérique du Nord (surtout l'Union Européenne, la Russie et les Etats-Unis).

4 LA REACTION DE LA PEUR

Wolfgang Bergsdorf professe l'opinion que, dans les sociétés libérales, la peur collective est un état menaçant qui peut déstabiliser et déséquilibrer le gouvernement.[22] Vu la politique antiterroriste actuelle en Amérique et en Europe, cette hypothèse de Bergsdorf est bien douteuse. Déjà, du point de vue contractualiste un tel point de vue est douteux et idéalise en plus les sociétés démocratiques comme étant sans peur.

Chez Hobbes, comme on l'a déjà montré, la peur est la raison principale pour quitter l'état belliqueux de nature et s'organiser en société. Par la démarche de sortie de l'individualisme isolé de l'état de nature, les hommes n'arrêtent pas seulement la guerre permanente entre eux mais ils seront à la fois constitués politiquement et rendus disponibles comme objets politiques. La peur les transforme en objets de décision de l'Etat. Cependant cet échange n'est point déraisonnable. Car les individus, même s'ils perdent leurs droits naturels et leur libre arbitre dans la décision, se voient en échange assurer l'existence et la vie. Même si la garantie de la survie est payée au prix de la liberté, ce n'est pas un mauvais échange.

Dans la perspective de Hobbes, la peur a, par conséquent, une double importance. La peur crée premièrement la motivation de sortir de l'état guerrier de nature et conduit deuxièmement vers un état de disponibilité politique de l'individu comme citoyen. Maintenant on pourrait bien sûr objecter que l'ordre social proposé par Hobbes n'est ni libéral ni démocratique. Mais le rapport constaté entre la fondation de l'Etat et la disponibilité politique des individus ne dépend pas de l'ordre social installé. La démarche consistant à échanger l'état de nature avec un état social est nécessairement liée à la disponibilité politique des individus, indépendamment de la question de savoir si les citoyens participent ou non à la législation.

22 Voir Bergsdorf (2000: 16, 19).

La mythologie de l'origine des sociétés modernes accorde à la peur une importance centrale de pouvoir disciplinaire. La connotation éthique positive de la peur dans les théories fondamentales des sociétés modernes ne reste pas - du point de vue politique - sans effets. A la différence des puissances impériales de l'antiquité ou de la pré-modernité, l'Etat constitutionnel moderne sait manier sa peur ouvertement. L'exemple, donné au début de l'analyse, de la Révolution française, exemple de vieille date, montre d'une part que la propre peur commence à devenir importante, mais aussi l'incertitude dans le traitement de la propre peur nationale. Si nous nous occupons de nouveau du problème du terrorisme transnational actuel, nous découvrirons dans les Etats menacés une politique de la peur beaucoup plus professionnelle.

Tenant compte de l'importance de la peur dans la théorie politique de l'Etat moderne on ne s'étonne pas que la raison principale donnée par les élites politiques pour une attaque guerrière soit la propre peur de l'Etat. L'argumentation avec la peur est très efficace. Indépendamment (on va se limiter à trois exemples), si l'administration Bush ordonne l'attaque de l'Afghanistan ou de l'Irak ou bien si le gouvernement de Vladimir Poutine exige une résolution militaire du conflit tchétchène, les activités militaires sont légitimées par l'argument d'une menace terroriste massive. Des conflits militaires sont menés au nom de la propre peur, quoique, à la différence des conflits territoriaux classiques, ce ne soit plus seulement la crainte d'un certain autre Etat qui soit le point central, mais c'est aussi cette peur diffuse et omniprésente du terrorisme qui sera politisée. Cela constitue un changement substantiel puisque ainsi la charge de la preuve des menaces - au moins de facto - sera renversée. Tandis que, dans la situation des conflits classiques (du moins de type idéal), on devait prouver que la crainte d'un ennemi défini et bien identifié est justifiée, le manque de sujet (personnel), propre à la peur du terrorisme, conduit à ce qu'on demande aux groupements et aux Etats soupçonnés qu'ils produisent la preuve de leur innocence. On peut l'exemplifier par la pression exercée sur la majorité des Etats de population musulmane, après le 11.09.2001, de se distancer publiquement de toute stratégie terroriste.

Présenter leur propre peur comme légitimation de leurs actions militaires, démontre aussi que le reproche que l'on fait souvent aux Etats Unis ainsi qu'à la Russie (pour la politique en Tchétchénie) de pratiquer une politique extérieure impériale anachronique, tenant compte du fondement légitimateur de cette politique, n'est pas fondé. Car l'impérialisme classique était caractérisé surtout par une stratégie de lutte contre la peur à l'intérieur du pays et par la volonté d'atteindre un climat courageux et un état sans peur. Les stratégies impériales, pré-modernes ou colonialistes modernes ne justifient jamais leur politique et leur désir expansionniste par leur propre peur.

Par contre, dans la stratégie du terrorisme transnational on peut constater une politique de la peur classique. Tandis que la ressource la plus importante du terrorisme réside dans la peur diffuse qu'éprouve son adversaire, la peur à l'intérieur de ses propres groupements de sympathisants, ainsi que dans leurs pays d'origine doit être minimisée.[23] Le terrorisme veut prouver et démontrer la vulnérabilité de son adversaire et ainsi diminuer la crainte vis-à-vis de l'ennemi. Car pendant que les stratégies antiterroristes attirent l'attention sur l'imprévisibilité, sur la menace terroriste et, par conséquent, insistent sur la grande force du terrorisme, la stratégie terroriste poursuit le but de démontrer la faiblesse de l'adversaire. Bien sûr une telle politique de la peur ne justifie pas de considérer finalement les stratégies terroristes comme impérialistes. Mais le fait que le terrorisme concentre sa politique de peur exclusivement vers l'extérieur, montre que les stratégies terroristes - en dépit de la modernité de leur tactique surtout psychologique - recourent aussi aux formes classiques de politique de guérilla.[24] Néanmoins, il faut retenir que, en ce qui concerne le rôle légitimateur de la peur, entre la stratégie terroriste et la lutte antiterroriste il n'y a pas d'équivalence structurelle.

Même si la stratégie terroriste de la peur d'une part, et la politisation de la peur dans les Etats menacés par le terrorisme d'autre part poursuivent des principes fondamentalement opposés, ils agissent en quelque sorte d'une manière complémentaire. Ainsi la peur provoquée par les attaques terroristes - par exemple dans la population américaine ou russe - peut être exploité pour légitimer une politique extérieure militaire. Le caractère de ressource de la peur se manifeste donc aussi dans les sociétés modernes. Que la peur soit considérée comme ressource aussi par les élites politiques des Etats modernes, ne se constate pas seulement dans son instrumentalisation pour certains objectifs de leur politique extérieure. De même le grand nombre d'Etats qui, au nom de leur propre peur du terrorisme transnational, ratifient l'extension des compétences dans le domaine de la sécurité intérieure, témoigne que la peur constitue une ressource qui présente de nouvelles possibilités et qui élargit les marges de manœuvre politiques. En plus, la peur est parfois reproduite systématiquement. La constitution du ministère pour la protection de la patrie aux Etats Unis et la création des degrés différents de sécurité nationale (code vert, jaune, orange, rouge)[25] sont seulement deux exemples que l'on peut mentionner ici.[26] Il faut

23 Par là, on ne peut bien sûr pas conclure que dans les pays d'origine des terroristes des attentats sont exclus.

24 Pour la distinction conceptuelle entre la guérilla et le terrorisme voir Waldmann (1998: 14 et suivantes).

25 Voir Barber (2003: 13).

26 A cause de l'ordre institutionnel américain, des telles mesures sont dans l'intérêt gouvernemental. Le système institutionnel des Etats Unis est fortement fédéraliste et se base sur une stricte séparation des pouvoirs. Dans ce système, le président joue un rôle assez faible en ce qui concerne la politique intérieure. C'est seulement en situation de crise particulière que le président dispose de larges compétences et d'un pouvoir étendu.

constater une tentative bien évidente de reproduire la peur en particulier eu égard à l'islam. Il est par exemple frappant que ce sont souvent les mêmes représentants politiques qui, eux-mêmes, ont un rapport très tendu avec l'égalité entre l'homme et la femme, l'homosexualité etc., qui attirent sans cesse l'attention sur les coutumes strictes de l'islam dans la hiérarchie des sexes ou dans la sexualité.

Quoique, pour le terrorisme, de même que pour les gouvernements des Etats menacés par le terrorisme, le caractère de ressource de la peur ait été démontré, on ne peut bien sûr pas conclure que les deux côtés agissent de manière concerté, qu'il soient dépendants l'un de l'autre ou qu'ils poursuivent le même but politique. Ni le gouvernement américain ni l'actuelle présidence russe n'a aucun intérêt d'être frappé dans sa propre population civile. On constate au contraire que des attaques terroristes répétées attirent la critique de leur lutte inefficace contre le terrorisme et, par conséquent, les gouvernements respectifs se retrouvent soumis à pression sur le plan politique.

On peut constater ainsi l'existence des stratégies de réduction de peur qui démontrent, à la fois, que les Etats nationaux - ayant une idée classique du conflit entre les pays, c'est-à-dire une idée inter-nationale - sont parfois dépassés par la structure moderne et complexe du terrorisme transnational. Une stratégie gouvernementale possible de limiter la peur consiste dans la réduction verbale de la complexité du terrorisme et dans la configuration verbale de l'ennemi terroriste. Une telle tentative de concentrer la peur diffuse dans la configuration définie d'un ennemi terroriste peut être retrouvée dans la notion El Keida. Il est possible que l'organisation d'Osama ben Laden forme un point important dans un réseau islamiste large et étendu, mais la considérer comme une entité fermée serait certainement une erreur.

Autrement que dans la stratégie terroriste, du point de vue des Etats menacés il peut y avoir, ainsi, une quantité trop grande de la ressource peur. Mais même si, comme on l'a déjà exemplifié, des attaques continuelles contre leurs populations va contre l'intérêt du gouvernement des Etats Unis et du gouvernement russe, la menace-même peut contribuer au renforcement du pouvoir. Car ce ne sont pas les attaques effectuées ni l'état de sécurité, mais bien la nécessité permanente d'éliminer le danger qui promet au gouvernement une liberté d'action exceptionnelle. La ressource de la peur peut ouvrir de nouvelles marges de manœuvre politiques surtout au cas où le gouvernement est capable d'offrir la sécurité.

5 CONCLUSION

Nous avons vu que déjà dans les fondements théoriques des Etats constitutionnels modernes, la peur est présentée comme une puissance politique centrale. Dans la mythologie hobbesienne des origines de l'Etat, la peur joue un rôle essentiel, motivant et justifiant la fondation de l'Etat. Par la création de l'Etat, les individus sont constitués comme citoyens et sont ainsi rendus politiquement disponibles. En ce qui concerne le problème du terrorisme globalisé et transnational, on a vu que l'étatisme théorique et méthodique du contractualisme offre seulement un faible potentiel d'explication. Mais en même temps, nous avons retrouvé la primauté théorique de la peur dans les conditions de la gouvernementalité transnationale moderne. Dans une modification moderne des principes de Hobbes, on pouvait constater que la peur ne règne plus seulement au niveau international, cela veut dire entre les Etats, mais que dans la situation du terrorisme transnational la peur des individus peut récupérer son importance politique. A la politique de la peur du terrorisme s'oppose une instrumentalisation de la peur par les gouvernements des Etats menacés. Malgré que la peur soit considérée par les deux adversaires comme une ressource politique, qu'elle soit exploitée et employée et qu'elle doive élargir et ouvrir des nouvelles marges de manœuvre politiques, les politiques de la peur se différencient, et cela pas seulement par leurs méthodes et par leurs buts. Il y a des différences importantes surtout en ce qui concerne la portée accordée à la peur à l'intérieur du propre groupe. Ainsi les stratégies terroristes poursuivent une politique classique de la peur par laquelle ils veulent provoquer la peur de l'adversaire tandis qu'ils combattent la peur à l'intérieur de leur groupe. Par contre, la politique de la peur des Etats menacés est dirigée surtout vers l'intérieur, et à cause de cela doit être catégorisée comme post-impériale.

Il reste encore à faire quelques observations. Dans notre analyse, il n'a pas été question - nous l'avons déjà mentionné - de la dimension psychologique individuelle de la peur. Au centre de l'intérêt figurait l'importance politique de la peur comme état collectif, à l'exemple du terrorisme transnational. Donc, quoique la peur ait été présentée dans son caractère de ressource, qui, bien sûr, dans les stratégies terroristes fonctionne autrement que dans la politique anti-terroriste des Etats menacés, on ne pourrait pas conclure que la peur, au niveau individuel, pût être infondée ou injustifiée. La structure transnationale et l'omniprésence tactique et stratégique du terrorisme sont sans doute effrayantes. Et surtout le manque de possibilité individuelle de prévenir les dangers donne l'impression d'une menace personnelle qu'on peut bien comprendre. Mais le fait que la peur du danger terroriste soit justifiée et comprise n'exclut pas sa (re-) production, sa politisation et son instrumentalisation et, par conséquent, son caractère de ressource. Il n'y a pas de conflit entre une critique de la politique de la peur, et la légitimité de la peur individuelle.

La peur réelle de la population n'est pas seulement fondée et justifiée, elle peut aussi être comprise comme signe d'un consensus général de la non-violence. Si on considère - pour en rester aux mêmes exemples - la société aux Etats Unis ou en Russie, la nécessité des élites politiques de mobiliser la peur de leurs populations pour légitimer des conflits militaires donne de l'espoir. Parce que si les stratégies militaires ne sont acceptées que sous la pression de la menace et de la peur, cela démontre le haut degré de l'esprit pacifique de ces sociétés.

Bibliographie

Arendt, Hannah, 1994, Macht und Gewalt. München, Piper.

Barber, Benjamin R., 2003, Imperium der Angst. Die USA und die Neuordnung der Welt. München, C.H. Beck.

Bergsdorf, Wolfgang, 2000, Politik und Angst: 13-28, in Franz Bosbach (dir.), Angst und Politik in der europäischen Geschichte. Dettelbach, Röll.

Czempiel, Ernst-Otto, 1999, Kluge Macht. Außenpolitik für das 21. Jahrhundert. München, C.H. Beck.

Foucault, Michel, 1975, Surveiller et punir. Naissance de la prison. Paris, Gallimard.

—, 1997, Die Sorge um sich. Sexualität und Wahrheit, Vol. III. Frankfurt am Main, Suhrkamp.

—, 1998, Der Wille zum Wissen. Sexualität und Wahrheit, Vol. I. Frankfurt am Main, Suhrkamp.

Heine, Peter, 2001, Terror in Allahs Namen. Extremistische Kräfte im Islam. Freiburg, Herder.

Hobbes, Thomas, 1998, Leviathan oder Stoff, Form und Gewalt eines kirchlichen und bürgerlichen Staates. Frankfurt am Main, Suhrkamp.

Hoffmann, Bruce, 2002, Terrorismus. Der unerklärte Krieg. Neue Gefahren politischer Gewalt. Frankfurt am Main, Fischer.

Jesse, Eckhard (dir.), 1996, Totalitarismus im 20. Jahrhundert. Eine Bilanz der internationalen Forschung. Bonn, BpB.

Kierkegaard, Sören, 1912, Der Begriff der Angst. Jena, Diederichs.

Lemke, Thomas, 2003, Andere Affirmationen. Gesellschaftsanalyse und Kritik im Postfordismus: 259-274, in Axel Honneth et Martin Saar (dir.), Michel Foucault. Zwischenbilanz einer Rezeption. Frankfurter Foucault-Konferenz 2001. Frankfurt am Main, Suhrkamp.

Neumann, Franz L., 1954, Angst und Politik. Tübingen, Mohr.

Putz-Osterloh, Wiebke, 2000, Angst und Handeln aus psychologischer Sicht: 1-11, in Franz Bosbach (dir.), Angst und Politik in der europäischen Geschichte. Dettelbach, Röll.

Seidelmann, Reimund, 1998, Kants „Ewiger Friede" und die Neuordnung des europäischen Sicherheitssystems: 133-180, in Klaus Dicke et Klaus-Michael Kodalle (dir.), Republik und Weltbürgerrecht. Kantische Anregungen zur Theorie politischer Ordnung nach dem Ende des Ost-West-Konflikts. Weimar, Böhlau.

Vasilache, Andreas, 2003, Interkulturelles Verstehen nach Gadamer und Foucault. Frankfurt am Main et New York, Campus.

—, 2005, Erklären und Verstehen bei Michel Foucault. In Rainer Greshoff et Georg Kneer et Wolfgang-Ludwig Schneider (dir.), Verstehen und Erklären. Eine Einführung in methodische Zugänge zum Sozialen. Stuttgart, UTB.

Waldmann, Peter, 1998, Terrorismus. Provokation der Macht. München, Gerling.

List of the authors

Pierre Bailly is Professor of Economics at the University of Pierre Mendès France de Grenoble.

David A. Dyker is Professor of Economics at the University of Sussex, Brighton. He is a member of the Academy of Learned Societies for the Social Sciences.

Olga Garanina is writing her doctoral thesis in Economic Sciences at the University Pierre Mendès France, Grenoble.

Aleksandr N. Nikolaev is Professor of Political Science at the State University for Economic and Social Sciences, Saratov.

Reimund Seidelmann is Professor of International Relations and Foreign Policy at the the Institute for Political Science at the Justus Liebig University of Giessen.

Andreas Vasilache is researcher and lecturer at the Institute for Political Science at the Justus Liebig University of Giessen.

Kirsten Westphal is Assistant Professor at the Institute for Political Science at the Justus Liebig University of Giessen.

Schriften zur Internationalen Entwicklungs- und Umweltforschung

Herausgegeben vom

Zentrum für internationale
Entwicklungs- und
Umweltforschung
der Justus-Liebig-Universität Gießen

Band 1 Hans-Rimbert Hemmer / Rainer Wilhelm: Fighting Poverty in Developing Countries. Principles for Economic Policy. 2000.

Band 2 Lorenz King / Martin Metzler / Tong Jiang (eds.): Flood Risks and Land Use Conflicts in the Yangtze Catchment, China and at the Rhine River, Germany. 2001.

Band 3 Ingrid-Ute Leonhäuser (ed.): Women in the Context of International Development and Cooperation. Review and Perspectives. Selected Papers and Abstracts presented at the Justus-Liebig-University Gießen 26.–28. October 2000. 2002.

Band 4 Margit Schratzenstaller: Internationale Mobilität von und internationaler fiskalischer Wettbewerb um Direktinvestitionen. 2002.

Band 5 Armin Bohnet u.a.: Theoretische Grundlagen und praktische Gestaltungsmöglichkeiten eines Finanzausgleichssystems für die VR China. Unter Mitwirkung von Chen Biyan, Chen Shixin, Ge Licheng, Ge Naixu, Ge Zhuying, Ma Shuanyou, Markus Peplau, Yang Zhigang, Zhu Qiuxia. 2003.

Band 6 Armin Bohnet / Matthias Höher (eds.): The Role of Minorities in the Development Process. 2004.

Band 7 Thi Phuong Hoa Nguyen: Foreign Direct Investment and its Contributions to Economic Growth and Poverty Reduction in Vietnam (1986–2001). 2004.

Band 8 Andreas Böcker / Roland Herrmann / Michael Gast / Jana Seidemann: Qualität von Nahrungsmitteln. Grundkonzepte, Kriterien, Handlungsmöglichkeiten. 2004.

Band 9 Christina Mönnich: Tariff Rate Quotas and Their Administration. Theory, Practice and an Econometric Model for the EU. 2004.

Band 10 Reimund Seidelmann / Ernst Giese (eds.): Cooperation and Conflict Management in Central Asia. 2004.

Band 11 Claudia Ohly: Das Steuersystem im ungarischen Transformationsprozess. Ein Beitrag zur Transformationstheorie. 2004.

Band 12 Nicole Mau: Umweltzertifikate. Der Einsatz von Umweltzertifikaten in der Landwirtschaft am Beispiel klimarelevanter Gase. 2005.

Band 13 P. Michael Schmitz (Hrsg.): Water and Sustainable Development. 2005.

Band 14 Ira Pawlowski: Die Wettbewerbsfähigkeit der ukrainischen Milchwirtschaft. Messung von Marktverzerrung und Politikeinfluß im Transformationsprozeß. 2005.

Band 15 Kirsten Westphal (ed.): A Focus on EU-Russian Relations. Towards a close partnership on defined road maps? 2005.